D1193287

ADVANCE R

Title: Cafe Life Florence: A Guidebook to the Cafés and Bars of the Renaissance Treasure

Author: Joe Wolff with photographys by Roger Paperno

Imprint: Interlink Books

Publication Date: September 2005

ISBN: 1-56656-562-6 • paperback $20.00 (in Canada, $27.95)

# of pages: 152 pages /full-color and b&w photography throughout

Size: 7" x 7"

Interlink Publishing Group, Inc.

46 Crosby Street, Northampton, MA 01060

Tel: (413) 582 7054 • Fax: (413) 582 7057

www.interlinkbooks.com

café life
FLORENCE

A Guidebook to the Cafés & Bars
of the Renaissance Treasure

Written by Joe Wolff
Photography by Roger Paperno

I

Interlink Books

First published in 2005 by

INTERLINK BOOKS

An imprint of Interlink Publishing Group, Inc.

46 Crosby Street, Northampton, Massachusetts 01060

www.interlinkbooks.com

Library of Congress Cataloging-in-Publication Data

Wolff, Joe.

   Café life Florence : a guidebook to the cafés and bars of the Renaissance City / by Joe Wolff ; photography by Roger Paperno.— 1st American ed.

      p. cm.

   ISBN 1-56656-562-6 (pbk.)

   1. Bars (Drinking establishments)—Italy—Florence—Guidebooks.

I. Paperno, Roger. II. Title.

   TX950.59.A-Z (Italy)

   647.9545'51—dc22   2004012084

Printed and bound in Korea

Book design by Juliana Spear

To request our complete 40-page full-color catalog, please call us toll free at **1-800-238-LINK,** visit our website at **www.interlinkbooks.com**, or write to **Interlink Publishing** 46 Crosby Street, Northampton, MA 01060 e-mail: info@interlinkbooks.com

LUNGARNO
CORSINI

CONTENTS

INTRODUCTION

*C*afé Life Florence is the second in the *Café Life* series, and, like its older sibling *Café Life Rome*, it profiles family-owned cafes, bars, and gelaterias and brings them to life. We started by talking to the owners and getting their personal stories; then we photographed them, their cafés, and their neighborhoods. Next, came the really hard part: exhaustive research that required careful sampling of fine espresso, exquisite gelato, and whatever other specialties were sold. (This went on day after day for weeks.) Finally, we compiled a list of 18 places in Florence that we like and hope you will, too. Some sell only gelato, others focus on chocolate, and still others offer a hybrid of goodies. Whatever their specialty, they have one thing in common—they're run by people obsessed with quality. They don't cut corners, and they're proud of it.

Count on the fact that every place selling coffee, or *caffè* as the Italians say, makes an excellent product with good Arabica blends. And the coffee menus are simple. So don't ask for a half-caf, low-fat, low-foam wet latte. The barista will look at you like you're *pazzo* (crazy). Keep it simple: espresso, cappuccino, macchiato. Also, it's a given that all gelato in this book is *gelato artigianale* (homemade gelato), not the *gelato industriale* sold by many tourist-trap gelaterias. The *artigianale* group makes the entire product from scratch and uses fresh fruit in the fruit flavors, while the *industriale* faction relies on a ready-made base and prepackaged flavoring. You really can taste the difference.

Since Florence is a renaissance treasure and *museo all'aperto* (open-air museum) that must be explored on foot, we chose strategically located places. No matter where you are, you'll find a good spot to refuel or take a break. Most are in the *centro storico*, some in the residential areas, and a few outside of Florence (in case you visit during the summer and want to escape the maddening crowds).

Use this book as your point of reference and organize your day around it because, in the end, a big part of the pleasure of Florence is experiencing its café life.

We would like to thank Alberto Pica of Gelateria Alberto Pica in Rome and Orazio Pomposi, owner of Badiani in Florence—without their invaluable help this book would not have been written. Joe would also like to thank his wife Robin Sloan for her support during the project.

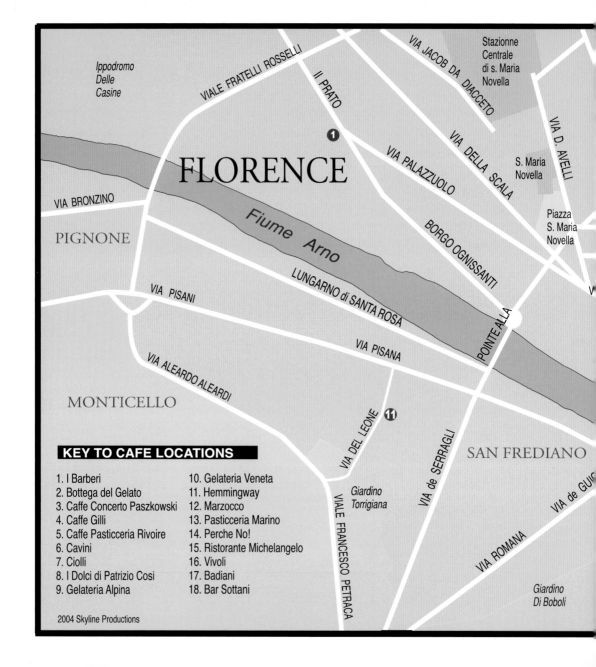

FLORENCE

Ippodromo
Delle
Casine

VIALE FRATELLI ROSSELLI

IL PRATO

VIA JACOB DA DIACCETO

Stazionne
Centrale
di s. Maria
Novella

VIA DELLA SCALA

VIA D. AVELLI

VIA PALAZZUOLO

S. Maria
Novella

VIA BRONZINO

Piazza
S. Maria
Novella

PIGNONE

Fiume Arno

BORGO OGNISSANTI

VIA PISANI

LUNGARNO di SANTA ROSA

POINTE ALLA

VIA PISANA

VIA ALEARDO ALEARDI

MONTICELLO

VIA DEL LEONE

VIA de SERRAGLI

SAN FREDIANO

VIA de GUIC

KEY TO CAFE LOCATIONS

1. I Barberi
2. Bottega del Gelato
3. Caffe Concerto Paszkowski
4. Caffe Gilli
5. Caffe Pasticceria Rivoire
6. Cavini
7. Ciolli
8. I Dolci di Patrizio Cosi
9. Gelateria Alpina

10. Gelateria Veneta
11. Hemmingway
12. Marzocco
13. Pasticceria Marino
14. Perche No!
15. Ristorante Michelangelo
16. Vivoli
17. Badiani
18. Bar Sottani

VIALE FRANCESCO PETRACA

Giardino
Torrigiana

VIA ROMANA

Giardino
Di Boboli

2004 Skyline Productions

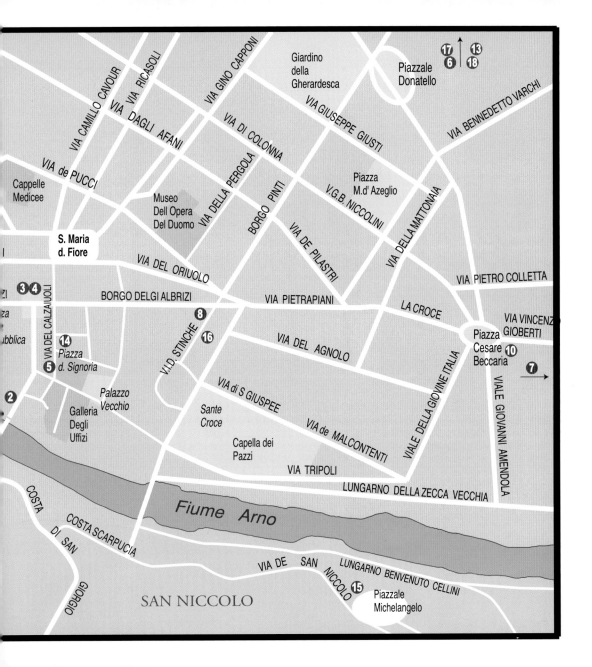

· 1 ·

CENTRO STORICO

little over half of the bars, cafés, and gelaterias in this book are in the centro storico*—defined by an area running from the Arno to Fortezza da Basso and Via Fiesolana to near Porta al Prato. This is probably where you'll spend most of your time, and all of our choices are in easy walking distance from each other. When you're looking for an address, remember the red numbers tend to be businesses and are usually written like this: 7/r. The concurrent blue or black numbers are residences (and often nowhere near the same number in red). Nothing is certain in Italy.*

I Barberi

Via Palestro at Via Il Prato
055 212604
Open 7AM—7PM, Monday
to Saturday
Closed Sundays

At the corner of Via Palestro and Via Il Prato sits an unassuming little bar that's full of surprises—from really good espresso and tasty made-to-order panini to the bright-eyed owner Signora Pinuccia Redditi (she goes by Pina).

The signora literally grew up in *ristorazione* (the food service and hotel business). She was born in 1944 in her grandmother's small albergo/ristorante in Montecatini Terme. The resort town, located a half-hour drive from Florence, is known for its curative spring-fed baths—people soak in the waters and take them internally as a liver restorative. "My grandmother was *molto in gamba* (very savvy). It was an important hotel before the war. People with money, and celebrities like Vittorio De Sica, went there," says Signora Redditi.

Vittorio De Sica (1901–1974) was a famous Italian actor and even more noted director: He won best foreign film Oscars for *Ladri di Biciclette* (The Bicycle Thief, 1949) and *Il Giardino dei Finzi-Contini* (The Garden of the Finzi-Contini, 1971).

"People from Varese and Milano came to Montecatini Terme. The town was very small in those days. It has grown a lot since then," says the Signora. "After the war, there was a *calo* (downturn). Business was not good because no one had any money, so my father came to Firenze, to the Piazza del Duomo, where he opened a restaurant called Da Pietro (his name was Pietro). He had it for 28 years. It's now a pizza place. After that, he bought a small hotel by the seaside."

The signora's father was the first in Florence to sell a ready-made sandwich. "Before he opened his restaurant in 1952," she continues, "he owned a *tavola calda* (snack bar) that specialized in pre-made *panini imbottiti* (sandwiches). In those days, you couldn't go into a bar and find a panino like this. Everyone copied him."

In 1985, she and her husband purchased a small bar on Via Il Prato and, after researching the history of the area, they decided to call it I Barberi. "I had to explain to everyone why I chose this name," she says. It refers to Berber horses—the fast, agile steed ridden by Berber warriors in AD 711 when the Arabs invaded the Iberian Peninsula. In Florence these animals ran a

riderless horse race called La Corsa Dei Barberi, starting at the nearby city gate called Porta al Prato and continuing down Via Il Prato past the current location of the bar. Prato means meadow, and in the early days of the race the street was an open field. The finish line was Piazza Beccaria, a distance of about three kilometers.

La Corsa Dei Barberi continued from 1200 to the late 1800s and was at its peak during the reign of Ferdinando I (1549–1609). He was one of the more popular Medici—a responsible and efficient ruler, as opposed to his ineffective older brother

Francesco I (1541–1587), who would rather experiment with alchemy and play with his pet reindeer than rule. The nobility watched the race from special stages strategically placed along the route, while the unwashed masses gathered in rough wooden grandstands or queued on the sidelines.

Almost every noble family competed in the race, and the wealthy Corsini were among the more successful. They had two palazzos—the largest one (never used) on Via del Parione had a hanging tapestry depicting their many trophies. A smaller, humbler abode, designed by the famous architect (and co-creator of gelato) Buontalenti, still exists on Via Il Prato. This palazzo was extended in the 1700s, and a special, long wooden balcony was built for watching the start of the race.

This same Porta al Prato where La Corsa dei Barberi began is also the starting point for the Scoppio del Carro, a splendid and oddball ritual. On Easter Sunday morning (around 9AM), a procession of drummers, soldiers, and incredibly skilled flag throwers in impeccable renaissance livery

leads the *carro*, a large wooden cart (resembling a wedding cake) pulled by four white oxen bedecked with flowers, to the Piazza del Duomo.

The *carro* is parked in front of the Duomo and a wire running from the altar is attached to its top. At approximately 11 AM, a smoldering mechanical dove races down the wire to ignite the fireworks on the *carro*. This is the *scoppio* (explosion), which continues as ring after ring of firecrackers explode in the air, filling the piazza with gun smoke. Not to worry: the oxen are led away before the fireworks begin, and Firenze's finest *vigili del fuoco* (firemen) stand by.

The story behind this tradition is a little vague. Apparently, it all started in 1097 when Pazzino de' Pazzi, a Florentine nobleman, joined the Crusades with a troop of 2,500 soldiers. They were the first to plant a Christian flag on the walls of Jerusalem, and, as a reward, Pazzi was given three pieces of stone from the Holy Sepulcher. He carried them back to Florence where they resided in the church SS Apostoli. The Pazzi family had the privilege of using the sacred stones as flint to light the traditional Easter fire.

It is not exactly clear when the *carro* first appeared—probably in the late 1300s. Lighting the mechanical dove with the sacred flint, as well as preparing the fireworks on the *carro*, also became part of the Pazzi job description. This duty continued until 1859 when the principle branch of the family died off and the city took over.

The current *carro* was built in 1765; and, since 1864, it has been housed in a garage on Via Il Prato with three-story-high wooden doors. As you face the Porta al Prato, it's on your right.

Signora Redditi has a photo of the bar's exterior taken in 1870 by the famous Alinari Brothers, who started the world's first photography business (photographers for hire) in 1852. They were commissioned by the Italian government to take official pictures of the new capital. "On the door you can see the words *coloniali* and *profumerie*," she says. "In those days the concept of a bar was different than today. The owner sold lots of things including *profumo* (perfume)… and *coloniali* (groceries)— products that came from the colonies like coffee, sugar, and tea. These were dispensed from huge containers by weight. You could get a caffé, but no panino like we have now. We still have the grocery license from those days, but we don't use it."

A few blocks from the bar on Corso Italia sits Teatro Comunale, a performing arts theater built in 1862 from a design by Telemaco Buonaiuti. Originally, it was *all'aperto* (in the open), then a roof was added in 1882. The theater holds about 2,000 people.

The theatre is the main site for the city's Maggio Musicale—a music festival running from May to July. Started in 1931, it's among the oldest music festivals in Europe. Zubin Mehta has been music advisor and chief conductor since 1986.

"In the summer, sometimes maestro Zubin Mehta comes in here. We get a variety of people," says Signora Redditi. "For example, there's Tom and Patricia from Washington. He's a university professor specializing in architecture of the Fascist era. Every other year he comes to Italy with a group of graduate students. He's a

good example of clients who've become good friends because they stopped in once and kept coming back. Sometimes they come to my house for dinner.

"There are two other Americans who are regulars. They live six months in Philadelphia and six months in Florence They own a beautiful apartment here. I think they have money, but they're very nice."

The United States Consulate is located a few blocks away on Lungarno Amerigo Vespucci. "The last two American consuls never came in, but before that two consuls in a row—two women—were regulars. Before she left, the last one gave me a beautiful book on the palazzi di Firenze as a gift. She's retired now, but she comes to Florence often and always stops to visit."

Signora Redditi's favorite story about celebrity visitors involves actor Matt Dillon and a bad case of indigestion. "Seven years ago, in 1996, he came in and he said to me, 'I don't feel well.' He spoke a little Italian. He'd eaten *pappa pomodoro* and *ribollita* at the same time. When I've eaten too much I take *citrosodina* (an antacid). You take two spoonfuls mixed in a glass of water. I gave this to him and he felt much better.

"I didn't recognize him at first, but then he removed his sunglasses… He has beautiful eyes. He'd gone to the men's fashion exhibition at Pitti Imagine as the guest of Giorgio Armani."

Many of the small old bars like I Barberi have disappeared over the years—some casualties of the 1966 flood and others victim of high rents and greed. Signora Redditi says at one time there were many small bars on Via Tornabuoni—now a designer row filled with high-fashion boutiques willing to pay exorbitant rents. But, the signora is positive about the future: "I think the small family bar and the *artigianale* approach to making things will not disappear. And there is support in the community. For example, the Principessa Corsini (from an old Florentine family of nobles who still owns a palazzo on Via Il Prato) puts on a *mostra artigianale* (artisan show). She believes in the artigiano Fiorentino."

After her husband died, Signora Redditi asked her son Riccardo, a sales rep in the Italian garment industry, if he wanted to work with her. He said, "I'll try it, and if I like it, I'll stay." So far, so good.

Come here for the coffee. For the panini. For the company of owner Signora Pina—a genuinely friendly and charming person. She's also a history buff, so if you speak Italian, she'll tell you about the rich past of her neighborhood. And if you don't parla Italiano *that's okay, too. She treats everyone the same, which is why you'll be welcomed like a regular after a few visits. And after a few more visits, you'll say,* "Questo è il mio bar"—*This is my bar.*

Bottega del Gelato

Via Por Santa Maria, 33/r
055 3296550
Open 7AM—9PM in winter
7AM—1AM in summer
Open daily

From *paracadutista* (paratrooper) to master *gelataio* (gelato maker), Sergio Brilli, owner of La Bottega del Gelato, has reached great heights in more ways than one. "I became a paratrooper in the *carabinieri* on a bet with a friend. I went as a joke and came out second in a class of 32 at jump school," says Brilli.

"It was very exciting. I liked it a lot, although the first time I was scared to death. You're jumping out of a plane at 700 meters. The worst jumps are at night, especially when there's no moon. Once, I hit the ground too hard because I didn't see it coming and didn't have time to pull up my legs. That's very dangerous—I could've been killed.

"I was the Lieutenant's orderly. Wherever he went, I was right behind him, carrying the radio. I was in for 15 months, attached to *un corpo speciale* (a special corps) based in Livorno that's called in case of emergencies. One time, I remember, during war games, we jumped over Siena and then returned, moving only at night. It took a week to get back to Livorno. It was a survival course.

"We got two salaries: one for being a *carabiniere* and one for being a paratrooper. That was another reason I did it—there wasn't much money in my family. When I finished my period of obligatory military service, the officials asked me if I wanted to stay, but I said no. I had a job waiting for me in Prato. Those were good times… I made a lot of friends. We still get together and have dinner."

Perhaps here is a good place for a couple of *carabinieri* jokes—for years the equivalent of dumb-blonde jokes in Italy. (In all fairness, the modern *carabinieri* is extremely efficient: It broke the back of the Brigade Rosse, and its antiterrorism and anti-Mafia units are first rate.)

While inspecting the barracks, a *carabinieri maresciallo* (a marshal or warrant officer) saw a corporal standing next to a light switch, turning it on and off, on and off. The maresciallo left and returned half an hour later. The corporal was still turning the switch on and off. The *maresciallo* said, "What are you doing? You're going to break the switch!" "No, *maresciallo*," was the answer. "It says right here…220 volt." (In Italian, *volte* means times.)

Why do you need 100 *carabinieri* to drive a nail? One to hold the nail, and 99 to pound on the wall.

Trading parachute silk for gelato was not a big leap for Brilli—his involvement in the bar/gelateria business actually began when he was a young boy. Born in Arezzo in 1949, Brilli was the oldest child in a large family that moved to Prato when he was 10, so his father (who worked in Florence and came home on weekends) could shorten his commute. Brilli cooked, made beds, and looked after the younger siblings, while his mother went out to clean houses. "At the age of 10, I also started cleaning and clearing tables in a bar," says Brilli. "I didn't have time for school or study. My family needed the money. In those days there was no compulsory education. Now you have to stay in school until you're 15."

"My first job was in a bar with the only TV in town. I was 8. I straightened the chairs, and the *signora* gave me hot tea and biscotti. One time in that bar, I found a thousand lire and took it home.

"I said, 'Mama, look I found mille lire.'

"'Take it back right away,' she said.

"'No, I found it on the ground.'

"'It doesn't matter...take it back where you found it.'

"So I took it back to the signora, and she gave me a 500 lire coin. I felt rich."

Little by little, Brilli moved from clearing tables to working as barista and finally to buying his own place—La Bottega del Gelato—in 1978. The first owner set up the gelateria and then a few months later, for some reason, sold it. "Before leaving, he taught me to make gelato," says Brilli, "and we continue to make it as we always have."

"We use only natural ingredients. They cost more, but the gelato is better and that's important. We make the gelato fresh every day—no preservatives. My strawberries are real strawberries, not flavored syrup or marmalade. When people taste my gelato, sometimes they say, 'This is really good. I'm not used to this.' That's because they eat artificial flavors most of the time.

"When we make melon ice cream, we put 2.5 kilos of melon in two *vaschette di gelato* (vats of gelato). This way you taste the real melon flavor. It's a real pleasure for me when a foreigner who was here years ago returns and finds the gelato is just like he remembered."

In 1980, Brilli found a woman to make the gelato so he could focus on running the business. "She's the best gelato maker in Florence," he says. "I don't know what I'll do when she retires in three years."

Originally, there was a very old bar/*tabacchi* at this location—part of the medieval city destroyed during World War II and later rebuilt. As Allied troops approached Florence after the fall of Rome in June 1944, the Germans realized it was time to leave town. On the way out, they blew up the bridges crossing the Arno along with the area around the Ponte Vecchio (old bridge), which included Via Por Santa Maria and the building containing the original bar/*tabacchi*.

The Germans evacuated 150,000 Fiorentini, and then at 10PM on August 3, 1944, the first of the mines set by a group of German paratroopers were detonated. Explosions continued until 5AM the following morning. When the smoke cleared, the only bridge standing was the Ponte Vecchio. Some say it was spared by the Führer, who loved Florence; others claim Field Marshall Kesselring simply refused to destroy the unique structure.

In spite of this reprieve, the Corridoio Vasariano sustained serious damage. The reason for constructing this private overhead passage, which was built in only five months during 1565 and runs along the top of Ponte Vecchio, was to get Cosimo I from Palazzo Vecchio to Palazzo Pitti void of contact with either the unwashed masses or his enemies. On August 5, 1944, the *partigiani* put the corridor to another use: They ran cable across its length to establish phone contact with the advancing allied army.

The Ponte Vecchio is more *vecchio* (old) than both the Palazzo Vecchio (built in 1315) and Cosimo il Vecchio (1389–1464), an early force behind the Medici's rise to power. Originally, there was a wooden bridge (dating from Roman times) at this narrowest point on the Arno within the city of Florence. By 1170, it was replaced with a stone structure that was later swept away during the terrible flood of 1333. The Ponte Vecchio, as we know it, was finished in 1345.

During the Middle Ages, the bridge was filled with blacksmiths, butchers, and tanners doing business from fire-prone wooden shops and using the river as a sewer. Each made his own personal contribution to the stench of the Ponte Vecchio. For the tanners, it was hanging hides in the river for seven or eight months and then curing them with horse urine.

Florence and its many bridges have always been threatened with floods—an unavoidable phenomenon of nature, as described in Francis Steegmuller's *A Letter from Florence*:

> First, the position of Florence is obviously a highly vulnerable one. At the bottom of a bowl of hills, it is watered by a river that during periods of rain and melting snow has always been swollen by tributaries from the deforested mountains among which it flows before reaching the city. One of these mountain tributaries, the Sieve, is particularly dangerous and has given rise to the Florentine proverb: *"Arno non cresce se Sieve non mesce"*—"The Arno doesn't rise unless the Sieve rushes into it." The only way to avoid Florentine floods, someone has said, would be to move Florence.

The great Leonardo da Vinci decided to take another approach. Instead of moving the city, he would divert the Arno. The main purpose was to make Florence a seaport and deprive rival city-state Pisa of its water supply, with the side benefit of creating a flood control system for the Arno valley.

Leonardo's plan was bold, and it failed big time. The government of Florence did not earmark enough money for the project, and it gave the contract to the lowest bidder, a hydraulic engineer named Colombino. Instead of following Leonardo's plan to dig one diversionary canal for the river, Colombino dug two. In addition, he tried to do it on the cheap—his 2,000-man crew completed the job in three weeks instead of six months, without building Leonardo's special digging machine as instructed. The ditches were too shallow and the river quickly resumed its old course. During this debacle, Leonardo was busy painting his mural of the Battle of Anghiari, inside the Palazzo Vecchio.

The worst flood of modern times took place in 1966. Early on November 4, a severe storm moved across Italy, dumping an incredible amount of water everywhere. The Arno rose 33 feet in 24 hours, overflowing its banks and flooding the city of Florence. Damage was horrific: every major piazza was under water; houses and palazzos were ruined, priceless art treasures destroyed. The numbers were staggering—39 people dead, 15,000 cars destroyed, 6,000 shops wrecked, 14,000 families homeless. The *centro storico* became a slimy sea of mud, debris, and heating oil, and still, nearly 40 years later, restoration work is far from over.

Again, Francis Steegmuller writes about the flood and the Ponte Vecchio in *A Letter from Florence*.

> These merchants (on the Ponte Vecchio) employed a private night watchman. At about one in the morning, he telephoned to the homes of those whom he could reach, and a number came, unlocked their shops, and filled their suitcases with what they could, the bridge trembling beneath them. Others, in the absence of any

official warning, thought that their watchman was exaggerating, and went back to sleep. The jewelers who did come had to leave quickly; the water was close, and, in addition to the trembling, there were frightening sharp reports, as though the bridge were cracking. The wife of one of the jewelers had said that when she and her husband arrived they found a number of noctambulous Florentines—some of them apparently hoodlums, some in cars with headlights pointed towards the scene—gathered at the end of the bridge, watching, as though hoping to see it break and collapse…The water continued to rise and about half the jewelry shops on the Ponte Vecchio are now gaping open—gutted by the tremendous force of a torrent that passed right through them.

In 1980, two years after Brilli purchased the gelateria, the Arno threatened Florence once again. He claims that he could reach over the side of the Ponte Vecchio and touch the water. "I was ready to evacuate," says Brilli. Fortunately, the river subsided.

It was during this period that Brilli and his wife Roberta worked night and day to keep the business going, while at the same time taking care of Tomasso, born in 1981.

"We used to bring him in here when he was a baby. He'd play with the little plastic spoons and pretend he was making gelato," says Brilli. "He went to university but didn't like it. Then he worked here with me for a year. Now he and his friend Jacopo Anzuini have started a *paninoteca* (sandwich bar). He's starting to appreciate the type of work I've been doing… the sacrifices involved. You have to work when you're sick with a fever, or when you just feel like staying in bed, because someone has to do it.

"I sent him to London a few times to study English. I thought this might help with whatever kind of work he did. My second son Andrea has also studied English… five years at a British school. My daughter Marta, who was born in 1990, is a ballerina, and she's been in a couple shows at the Teatro Verde."

For the first eight years they had the business, Brilli and his wife Roberta did not have a vacation. She doesn't work anymore and life has gotten a little easier—for a month every year the family goes to the seaside for a vacation. He joins them for a week.

"I'm 54 years old and I've worked for 43 years. I came from nothing. I'm lucky to have good health and an exceptional family. When I come home, my children come to meet me, my wife greets me, the dog greets me. It's nice," Brilli says with a smile.

On your way to the Ponte Vecchio, you'll most likely pass Bottega del Gelato. It has a rather plain exterior, but as the old saying goes: Don't judge a gelato by its cone. Go inside and try Sergio Brilli's marvelous gelato cioccolato, *his homemade frozen yogurt or* gelato di soya *(soy gelato without sugar for diabetics). He also makes an excellent cup of coffee, which as Brilli says, depends on good water, good beans—and the hand of the barista. The* panini *aren't bad either. You might also visit his son Tomasso's* paninoteca, L'Verrocchio, Via A. del Verrocchio, 2r, 055 2480680, near Mercato di Sant'Ambrogio.*

Caffé Concerto Paszkowski

Piazza della Repubblica, 6/r
055 210236
Open 7AM—1:30AM, Tuesday to Sunday
Closed Mondays

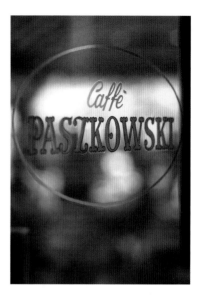

As you traverse Piazza della Repubblica, you'll notice busy, high-profile Caffé Paszkowski and Caffé Gilli (see next listing) and you may think they're cold, efficient places owned by large corporate entities, much like Café Doney, Café De Paris, and Caffé Greco in Rome. But they're not. The Valenza family is the proprietor of both establishments and, because of this, each has the warmth generally associated with smaller mom-and-pop cafes.

The early history of Caffé Paszkowski is a little vague, though this much is clear: In 1846, it was founded as a brewery and beer hall at its present location by a Polish gentleman named Paszkowski. His intention was to teach the Italians how to drink beer.

By the turn of the century, Caffé Paszkowski (or Pazzoschi as the Fiorentini nicknamed it) had morphed from a beer hall into an elegant hangout for artists, writers, and musicians—especially the Futurist crowd. This included Giuseppe Prezzolini, founder of the literary review *La Voce* (1908–1910), along with Giovanni Papini, poet, novelist, and historian, and his colleague, writer and painter Ardegno Soffici, who started another literary review called *Lacerba* (1913–1915). Futurism was an Italian arts movement that embraced the changing world of the 20th century—its followers were into war, noise, speed, machines, cities, and the nationalistic right wing.

No surprise that Mussolini sniffed around this group: Many contend Fascism had it roots in here.

When Piero Valenza took over the business in 1979, it was in bad shape—little more than a glorified cafeteria for tourists. He transformed it into a respectable restaurant; began making homemade bread, pastry, and gelato; and reinstituted the outdoor concert series. Paszkowski came back to life like a reclaimed wetland and, with its former grandeur restored, the Fiorentini returned.

As a young *carabiniere* from Sicily, Valenza was stationed first in Torino and then Florence, where he met his wife Linda, who was a seamstress from a poor Emilia-Romagna family. They were both 21 years old.

"When they met, they had nothing," says daughter Sonia, 33, "but their love was very strong. My father decided to leave the *carabinieri* after seven years of service. He was looking for something more, so he became a middleman, or agent, for buying and selling businesses. He made some money and bought a place called Caffè New York. He began doing really well during the '60s. There was an economic boom… tourism skyrocketed. And little by little, he and my mother built up an empire.

"He was born a business man. He had business in his soul. He'd lie awake at night trying to figure out ways to buy another business… make more money. And he was not afraid to lose, but very *scaltro* (shrewd). He slept little and lived hard, which contributed to the fact that he died in 1995 at the young age of 54, from a liver ailment."

Entrepreneurial, driven, talented—Piero Valenza owned seven cafés at the time of his death. The family kept three: Paszkowski, Gilli, and Gran Caffè Rondo (in front of the Battistero del Duomo). "I lost my father when I was 20. It was a shock… it changed everything. Little by little, we recovered," says Sonia's 30-year-old brother Marco. Sonia, who is very focused and articulate, manages Gilli; Marco runs Paszkowski; and their mother acts as a consultant.

"We were more or less born in these places," continues Marco, "my sister in '69, me in '73, and we grew up in them. But our parents always let us choose our life, our own address, so to speak. Eventually, this work became a passion for me and my sister. She specializes in chocolates, confections, and display. My area is wine."

Marco lights up when he talks about wine—what started as a hobby after completing a sommelier course grew to a passion. The ever-growing wine list at Paszkowski reflects this with bottles from France, Italy, South Africa, New Zealand—and more than 70 different Brunellos, plus many vintages from small Tuscan wineries. The type of list you would expect to find in the finest of restaurants, not a café.

It's in the area of wine that Marco reminds Sonia of her father: He's energetic, with big plans. "I love the world of wines because it is an infinite world," says Marco.

When he has spare time, which is rare, he likes to play soccer. He also enjoys music; everything from American hard rock to classical. He even dabbles in playing the drums and knows one of the U2 drummers who brought the superstar Bono around for a drink one evening.

In Italian bar/café/gelateria circles, Caffé Paszkowski's name is well known. For that reason, it was "borrowed" by a café on Piazza Matteotti in Udine. By chance, one of Sonia's customers came up to her and said, "I see that you opened a Paszkowski in Udine."

"Not that I know of…" replied Sonia.

Her client told her, "The name is spelled the same, with the same logo."

She immediately went to Udine with her fiancé, pretending that the two of them met at the original Paszkowski in Florence and were surprised to find another one in Udine. The owners began talking about how they were family members.

Then came the moment of truth: "I told them who I was, and if they didn't stop using our name I was going to contact a lawyer," she said. "It was a small cafeteria. They didn't really cause any long-term harm. I guess they figured we wouldn't sell the rights so they just took them. It was incredible."

Of the two cafés run by the Valenzas, Paszkowski has the more masculine feel (maybe it's the beer hall roots). It has a complete restaurant menu with an excellent wine list. The "Concerto" in the name refers to the fact that there is live music every evening from 9pm to 1am—outside in the summer and inside at the piano bar in the winter.

Caffé Gilli

Piazza della Repubblica, 39/r
055 213896
Open 8AM—midnight, Wednesday to Monday
Closed Tuesdays

Originally, Caffé Gilli was founded by a Swiss family named Gilli in 1773 on Via Calzaiuoli as a *bottega dei pani dolci* (sweet bread shop) that sold pastry to the nobles. In 1848, it moved to Via Speziali, occupying the space where the Hugo Boss store now stands. The business changed hands in 1890, purchased by the Frizzoni, another Swiss family, and transferred to Piazza Vittorio Emanuele (changed in 1946 to Piazza della Repubblica).

When the piazza's original namesake united Italy in 1865, Florence became the capital of the Italian Republic, which meant big changes for the city of 100,000. Overnight, it had to absorb the 15,000 people who made up the new government bureaucracy. There was a shortage of living space and rents skyrocketed. The city built temporary prefab structures of wood and steel on the outlying areas.

Architect Giuseppe Poggi (see Ristorante Michelangelo) submitted a controversial 50-year plan, which set the tone for urban development. The city fathers put it into execution immediately. Old city walls were pulled down (north of the Arno) and replaced by *viali*, avenues, interspersed with two open spaces—

Piazza della Libertà and Piazza Beccaria. Parks and gardens were constructed and permanent housing built on undeveloped land inside the city walls.

In 1870, the capital abruptly moved to Rome. Yet somehow this did not slow the momentum of the re-development frenzy. Poggi's plan included part of an earlier plan by an architect named Del Sarto to rebuild the *centro città* (city center). The city fathers still thought this a great concept and decided to gut the heart of Florence—an area bordered by Via dei Calzaiuoli, Via Porta Rossa, Via dei Pescioni, and Via dei Cerretani. (Unfortunately, the speculative mentality is not limited to the present; it was alive and well in Florence during this period.)

In the late 1800s, the center was a rabbit warren of medieval streets, which included the ghetto and a very old, colorful area of the city called the Mercato Vecchio (old market)—built on the site of the ancient Roman forum, which stood at the intersection of Cardo and Decomanus, the two principal streets of the Roman colony Florentia. During a typical day at the Mercato Vecchio in the 1300s, you'd find one of everything, from doctors and apothecaries to silk merchants, magicians, and deformed beggars.

Many Fiorentini did not want either the crowded ghetto or an old marketplace in what they thought should be the most elegant part of town. So, in 1885, the ghetto and all buildings around Mercato Vecchio were razed, along with the homes of old Florentine families such as the Medici and Sacchetti, and the area was enlarged to form Piazza Vittorio Emanuele. Only Vasari's fish market survived, moving to Piazza dei Ciompi.

Gilli opened its doors at the present location, on the ground floor of a building owned by a large insurance company, about the time redevelopment was completed. One hundred years later when Piero Valenza bought the business, it was struggling. "The previous management let it go downhill," says Sonia Valenza. "It was little more than a *tavola calda* (cafeteria). Many historical businesses like this were considered only tea rooms, but they had a lot more potential... my father

saw this. He formed a *società* (corporation). He had 45 percent ownership, and three days after the sale, he bought out his partners. He moved very fast."

As for Sonia herself, when she's not at Gilli, she works in her garden and plays with her six dogs—a Maltese named Kicko, a pair of Great

Danes named Greta and Otone, and their three sons, Lordo, Jerry, and Pongo. She also enjoys dancing, which she has studied since she was small. "It helps me clear my mind," she says. And, whenever possible, she spends time with her fiancé Claudio, a singer who travels quite a bit. They met at the San Remo music festival in 2001.

Does anyone you know come to Gilli? Julia Roberts and Bono have eaten here, but not together. The well-known *cantautore* (singer-songwriter) Adriano Celentano stops by, as well as Renato Zero, a very famous Roman singer.

There is an episode with Renato Zero that Sonia likes to tell: "He came in one day and asked for a table. Everyone was nervous… they wanted to give him good service. He's very popular here. In his strong Roman dialect, with a sweeping gesture, he ordered a *ventaglio*—a type of fan-shaped pastry. This word also means fan in Italian. The confused waiter went out and bought a real fan and served it on a little porcelain plate. Whenever Renato Zero returns, he laughs about the ventaglio."

One time, Vittorio Gassman, the late stage and film actor, accidentally bumped his head on the frosted glass door of an inside door and broke it. The famous "hole by Gassman" remained for many years because of the difficulty of finding special replacement glass.

Gilli has been a location for the TV show *Colpo Di Fulmine* (Bolt of Lightning), a sort of Italian Dating Game, and many Italian films were shot here as well, including *Donne Con Le Gonne* (women with gowns), the story of a brutish husband who imprisons his wife in order to dominate her. It stars Francesco Nuti, well known in Italy as both an actor and director.

At the end of the day, both Sonia and Marco depend on their mother for support and advice. "My mother is a rock… very intelligent in every sense," says Sonia. "She taught us how to handle life and its difficulties. My father was more calculating. More of a dealer. A horse trader. It's a good balance."

Prices are steep at both Paszkowski and Gilli, but worth paying to rent a table outside for the afternoon to watch both your fellow patrons and the parade of humanity through Piazza della Repubblica.

Gilli is an elegant coffee shop that makes its own excellent chocolates and pastries— try the famous Tuscan cantuccini (biscotti) soaked in vin santo. You also might want to visit the outside corner of the café nearest Via Roma, which is the exact spot where a young woman walked the gauntlet of leering Italian men in the incredible photo American Girl in Italy *taken by Ruth Orkin in 1951.*

Caffé Pasticceria Rivoire

**Via Vacchereccia, 4
(Piazza della Signoria)
055 214412
Open 8AM—midnight,
Tuesday to Sunday**
Closed Mondays

Although the Bardelli brothers (Antonio, Bruno, Aurelio, and Hugo) have done well in a very difficult business, their beginning was shaky—and damp. Three months after they opened their first location, Bar Orologio on Via Por Santa Maria near the Ponte Vecchio, the *alluvione* (big flood) hit.

"It was November 4, 1966. We went to the bar at 8AM," says Bruno Bardelli, a precise, friendly man. "The water was already beginning to rise. At 8:15, suddenly we felt a *grande schianto* (big crash) against the window. An *argine* (dyke) near the Ponte Vecchio broke and water came in a wave. We managed to escape to our house on Via del Ponte alle Mosse—to the third floor. From the window, we saw tree trunks, wardrobes, furniture—everything flowing by in the strong current. The area near us was low-lying and many people lived on the ground floor. As the water rose, they went from the ground to the first floor and from there to the roof. We could see them on their rooftops yelling for help.

"It lasted five to six hours. About noon or one o'clock, the water began to subside. We returned to our bar late in the evening and it was a mess. Counters, chairs, tables, food, had been under water... all ruined. We were terribly discouraged. This was the moment of crisis. Should we abandon our bar or begin again?

"We got lots of encouragement and help from friends and family. So, the next morning, we began to clean up. For 15 days, we removed mud—it was everywhere. The fire department also helped. Then, under very difficult circumstances, we opened for business. There was no glass in the counter and the espresso machine was on an improvised

stand. Eventually, we recovered and things began to go well for us."

In 1968, they bought another bar in Via Calzaiuoli and sold their original business, Bar Orologio. Other bars they've owned include Bar Due Punti on the Lungarno degli Acciaiuoli, Bar Cristallo on the Piazza della Stazione, and Café Giacosa on Via Tornabuoni, which they kept until 2000.

"We worked with a partner only once, in a pasticceria on Borgo Ognissanti, but left after a year. There were some problems and we were more used to working our own way," says Bruno. "Over the years, we've moved from one place to another, always trying to improve the quality, the ambiance, the name. After selling Giacosa,

we've arrived at a point of *tranquillità* (tranquility). We don't want to keep growing. We're going to stop with Rivoire and enjoy what we have."

The story of Rivoire began in 1872 when Enrico Rivoire came to Florence, the capital of Italy, and opened a chocolate factory at the present location. The origin of his last name is not certain—probably from a French family that relocated to Turin. Anyway, Rivoire learned his craft in Torino, which was the center of chocolate making in Italy and home to businesses such as Perugina.

At first, the small, steam-powered factory made bulk chocolate and served cups of hot chocolate at an inside counter. Gradually, it expanded, taking over half of the bottom floor of Palazzo Lavison—constructed between 1858 and 1870 during the somewhat ruthless redevelopment boom in the heart of Florence (see Caffé Gilli).

At the turn of the century, when the outside of the palazzo was renovated, Rivoire added outdoor tables. The business remained in the family until 1978.

Originally, it was not the Bardelli Brothers' idea to buy Café Rivoire. "In 1977, the niece of Enrico Rivoire contacted us through an intermediary to see if we were interested," says Bruno Bardelli. "The Rivoire family felt it was time to sell. They knew many people were interested, but the niece didn't want to sell to someone who might change the café to a pizzeria. The uncle left them this patrimony and they wanted to make sure the new owner would honor it. They knew us from our business and our reputation.

"We had a meeting with the niece and her husband, and we promised that if we bought the place, we'd do everything possible to continue the tradition. For us, when we say something, we mean it. Our word is important.

"The family was very generous in selling the bar to us. We became the owners in 1978 and we have not betrayed their trust. We make the chocolate like they did in 1872. We wrap the chocolate by hand… everything is just as it was."

Since Rivoire is located on Piazza della Signoria, the civic center of Florence, you should know what you're viewing as you sit at an outdoor table and survey the scene. Here are the highlights.

The Piazza, named after the Signoria, the city's ruling council, was built at the end of the 1200s, and enlarged during the 1300s to its present "L" shape. It has always been the political heart of Florence and a place where many things happened—from games of *calcio storico* (a very old form of soccer) to the prudish Dominican monk Girolamo Savonarola's (1452–1498) huge "Bonfire of the Vanities." He invited the entire populace to throw their sinful possessions into the flames—only to find himself tossed into a bonfire four years later, roasted on the very same spot. Look for the round marble plaque on the ground near the equestrian statue of Cosimo I de' Medici by Giambologna that marks the exact location of Savonarola's incineration.

The original name of Palazzo Vecchio (constructed between 1299–1315) was Palazzo della Signoria—it was the seat of government from which the ruling council dispensed its sometimes questionable wisdom and from which the Medici later ran things with iron fists from 1500–1509. Cosimo Il Vecchio did some major redecorating, changing the feel of the building from fortress to comfortable residence. It is still the town hall of Florence.

In front of the Palazzo Vecchio sits the Fountain of Neptune by Ammannati and a copy of the David. As you face the palazzo, on the right side is the open-air Loggia dei Lanzi, a gallery-like structure with a number of art works including Giambologna's sculpture *Rape of the Sabines* (1583) and Cellini's bronze *Perseus* (1554).

If you were around at the time the Fiorentini were building Palazzo Vecchio, you would have paid for things with gold florins, minted from 3.53 grams of 23-carat gold. The coin was first issued in 1252 by the Republic of Florence and soon became the international monetary standard (the US dollar of its day). Instead of Washington, Jefferson, or FDR, it had St. John the Baptist on the front with the Florentine *giglio* (lily) on the reverse side. St. John, the patron saint of Florence, was chosen because he was considered a straightforward and no-nonsense person (like the Fiorentini themselves). He said things such as: "Exact no more than that which is appointed to you"; "Do violence to no man, neither accuse any falsely: and be content with your wages"; and, "He that hath two coats, let him impart to him that hath none; and he that hath meat let him do likewise."

Many films have used Piazza della Signoria as a location—the most notorious of recent years being the gratuitously violent *Hannibal* (2000). Chief Inspector Rinaldo Pazzi of the Questura played by Giancarlo Gianinni is disemboweled as he is hung from an upper window in the piazza, the same punishment meted out to his distant relative Francesco de' Pazzi for murdering one of the Medici. "During filming they closed the piazza," says Bruno Bardelli, "but usually they shot late at night or early in the morning, so it didn't bother us."

Some of Rivoire's more well-known European customers include Sandro Pertini (1896–1990), popular socialist president of Italy from 1978–1985, who came for the hot chocolate. He took office a few months after Aldo Moro's body was found in the trunk of a car in downtown Rome—this was at the height of *gli anni di piombo* (the years of terrorism in Italy). Pertini, though, was no stranger to upheaval. Exiled to France from 1926–1929 for being anti-fascist, he returned to Italy and was promptly arrested and served eight years in prison. He later fought with the *partigiani* against the Germans until 1944, when he was captured and sentenced to death by the SS. Miraculously, he escaped.

Fabiola, the Spanish-born Queen of Belgium, stops by for lunch when she is in town. The descendant of an aristocratic family, she worked as a nurse in Madrid before marrying King Baudouin on December 15, 1960. The King died in 1993. Throughout her life, Fabiola has supported medical and social charities for children, and she even donates royalties from her children's storybook, *Twelve Marvelous Tales of Queen Fabiola*, to the Belgian National Children's Charity.

Many people have proposed the idea of opening a second Caffé Rivoire in Japan or New York, but the brothers remain adamant in their rejection of this idea. As Bruno Bardelli puts it, "This would make us *industriale* (big business) and we would lose the *artigianalità* (craftsmanship and originality)."

Whether you sit inside or outside, Café Rivoire is a good place to go for a splurge. The specialty is chocolate—so go for it with a cioccolata in tazza *(hot chocolate in a cup). Try some pralines from their excellent bakery or a cup of their very good cappuccino. When the weather is sunny, it's best to park yourself at an outdoor table and watch the human zoo on parade in the Piazza della Signoria.*

I Dolci di Patrizio Cosi

Borgo degli Albizi, 15/r
055 2480367
Open 7AM—8PM, Monday to Saturday
Closed Sundays

*B*efore you visit this pasticceria for an excellent pastry and a fine espresso, you should put things in perspective (architecturally speaking, that is). First, locate the tiny Piazza San Pier Maggiore just off Borgo degli Albizi, then find the Via San Pier Maggiore running off the piazza. This narrow street goes right through the front door of what used to be a church and convent called the Convento di San Pier Maggiore—look closely and you'll see the portico. The Benedictine convent and its church extended from the piazza all the way to the post office on nearby Via Giuseppe Verdi.

Now walk along Borgo degli Albizi a short way to Piazza Gaetano Salvamini. On the right, you'll see remnants of the church's bell tower built into a *palazzo* (building) containing shops and apartments—look for the two matching lion heads.

Like many churches, San Pier Maggiore was originally built (around 1050) outside the city walls, and the *borgo*, or village, that sprung up around it took its name—Borgo di San Piero. When the city walls were later rebuilt to include these small enclaves, the local street retained the name of the borgo. Some examples are Borgo Ognissanti, Borgo Santi Apostoli, and

Borgo San Frediano. In the case of the street called Borgo di San Piero, its name was changed to Borgo degli Albizi by the wealthy Albizi family who built a palazzo at #12 and did pretty much whatever they wanted.

The Convento di San Pier Maggiore was torn down in the 1700s—today only the façade, the bell tower, and a few other parts of the original structure remain intact. Il Duce wanted to raze this whole area to make room for a boulevard running from the periphery of Florence to the *centro storico*, but, as happened with similar situations in Rome, the project was halted by strong protests from the locals.

After World War I, the building that replaced the church and convent was used as a barracks and later converted to the apartments you see today. About halfway down this building on Borgo degli Albizi you'll see the entrance to Patrizio Cosi's pasticceria. Once inside, take a moment and realize—you're actually standing in the middle of a former convent built 1,000 years ago. This reflection will give your brioche a definite historical (and religious) flavor.

Depending on the time of day, the owner may be there. You can't miss him; he's the pleasant-looking little man with an infectious laugh and a twinkle in his eye, as if he knows an inside joke and he may let you in on it.

"I come to work at 3:30 in the morning. I leave at 1:30PM and then come back at 4 in the afternoon," says Patrizio Cosi. "I don't need to sleep. There was a time, though, when I was tired… when I was about 35," he continues. "Now I turn off the alarm before it rings and get up. Three hours at night and then an hour in the afternoon is enough sleep for me. I go to bed about midnight.

"I have a daughter Anna, who's 27… when she was little, I never saw her. She was always asleep when I got home, and when I went to work. This is a difficult job if you have a family."

Cosi employs four workers in his *laboratorio* (kitchen): two in the day and two in the evening. The evening workers are the beginners—people who want to learn the trade. When a morning person leaves, Cosi moves up an evening person. This system provides him with a built-in apprentice program and a steady supply of properly trained *pasticcieri* (pastry makers). "I don't want to hire an experienced pasticciere. I want people who don't know anything so I can train them to do things my way. The thing is, those who already have their way don't want to change."

Now Patrizio Cosi has a young Japanese man and woman working the day shift in the *laboratorio*. He likes to employ them because he says they want things to be precise and beautiful. The young man has been with him two years and the young woman for three years. Originally, she was a regular customer, who one day said, "I'd like to work here."

"They speak good Italian. And when you give them something to do, they do it," says Cosi. "Italians always want to change procedures… be creative… do it their way. It's good to be inventive, but not here. I already have my way of doing things and it works well. The Italians also want to know, 'How much am I going to earn.' I say, 'Let's see what you can do, and then we'll discuss salary.'"

Patrizio Cosi does not come from a long line of pastry makers. In fact, he learned the trade on his own initiative by apprenticing himself as a 14-year-old boy to a Florentine master. Cosi says, "I came from less than nothing and I created this myself." He's been making pastry for 38 years. "The secret to making good pastry is balance," he says. "Not too sweet, not pretentious, not too much fat… natural ingredients and a classic approach. Everything is complicated today. It's only complicated because people make it that way. Good pastry is not complicated. It's simple. You use fresh ingredients every day. From fresh ingredients, you get a fresh product. Everyone likes it."

Crema pasticceria (custard) is an important element in many of Patrizio Cosi's creations. He religiously makes his *crema* the old-fashioned way using his own recipe, which is, of course, simple. A *paiolo di rame* (copper pot), fresh milk and eggs, some sugar—mix slowly.

"In most bakeries when you taste the custard, you taste powdered milk because they make it with a pre-made mix in huge 50-liter cauldrons. That is an industrial product. Mine is not," says Cosi.

Cosi has been in this *pasticceria* (his fourth) since 1985. During its lifetime, the location has also been home to a butcher shop, a chocolate shop, and a paint store.

He enlarged the space when he took it over—a bureaucratic nightmare of the first order. After getting special work permits from the city because of the location's historical significance, he began construction, and was then suddenly told to stop.

For two years he beat a path to city government offices in the Palazzo Pitti, trying to get the missing permits. At one point, he says, "*Mi sono incavolato* (I lost my temper)," and his name went to the end of the list. Luckily, he found someone with connections; within a few days, he got what he needed.

The *pasticceria* is flourishing, and Cosi has come a long way from his life as the son of a poor *contadino* (farmer)." I worked in the fields until I was 14, taking care of the olive trees and harvesting crops. My father worked the farm for the owner. Half of what you grew was yours and the other half was his—they call it *mezzadria* (sharecropping). We also got a house rent free… it was another world then. Sometimes we'd sell chickens and rabbits so we could buy pants and shoes. I'm grateful that I had a life like that—it helped me appreciate what I have now," says Cosi.

"The young Italians of today don't appreciate anything, and it's our fault because we've given them everything. They go to school until they're 30 and they don't know anything. They're called *dottore*, but they don't have any work. Better if they're called *contadino* and have some work."

Try anything made with Patrizio Cosi's special custard, especially the millefoglie *and* torta della donna. *It's ironic that a pleasure dome of pastry like I Dolci di Patrizio Cosi sits on a spot once occupied by the ascetic Convento di San Pier Maggiore. Check out the bagno (bathroom) in the corner—there is an original main column from the convent's church rising into the apartment directly above.*

Gelateria Alpina

Viale Filippo Strozzi, 12/r
(Fortezza da Basso)
055 496677
Open 6:45AM—9PM in winter
6:45AM—midnight in summer
Closed Tuesdays

*I*n the summer, they were migrant *gelatai* (gelato makers) and in the winter, mountain people. This was the life of many miners, farmers, and artisans hit hard by the economic downturn of the late 1800s in the Val di Zoldo region of the Veneto. They headed north to Vienna and sold roasted chestnuts, caramel apples, and pears—and eventually *gelato artigianale* (homemade ice cream). In fact, around 1870, two Italians from Val di Zoldo got the first license to make and sell gelato in Vienna.

And it was not just Val di Zoldo. From all over the Veneto, gelato makers migrated to every corner of the world: America, Germany, Argentina, Switzerland, Peru, Canada, Japan, and China.

The movement continued well into the 1920s, when Giovanni De Rocco's grandfather went looking for work. "After World War I, my *nonno* (grandfather), Giovanni Arnoldo, lived in Czechoslovakia. Then he returned to Italy and saw that Florence might be a good market for gelato because at the time there were few gelaterias here. He came to Florence in 1922 with two brothers and opened Gelateria Veneta (still in existence and also in this book). They eventually split up and brother Virgilio opened Gelateria Alpina in 1929.

"At that time, the business was seasonal—they were here from the middle of March to the first of September. Then they closed up shop and went to the mountains to hunt and chop wood. People from that area are charming and playful, but more *chiuso* (reserved) than Romans. *Piu si sale, piu ci si chiude* (The further north you go, the more reserved you are).

"The gelateria is still family-run, passed from my grandfather's brother to my father, then to me in 1967. Next is my son and we hope, some day, my grandchildren," says De Rocco, a well-knit, middle-aged man who looks like someone who has spent time hiking and rock climbing. The family still has a home at Forno di Zoldo in the Dolomites (where he lived until the age of 9), and he gets out into the mountains as often as possible.

He'll tell you he was born into a business that gives him *soddisfazione moralmente* (moral satisfaction), which is not something you hear every day from a business man.

"At some point in life, you have to decide: Is it quality I'm going after or quantity? I chose quality. Quantity diminishes the quality. My father and grandfather and his brothers made the same choice. When you make a product at a high level, your customers appreciate it. That can be more satisfying than money."

Creating the best gelato on the planet can be tricky because this frozen delight is temperamental. You need the hygienic equivalent of a clean room, the finest ingredients, an old family recipe, and just the right touch. And then you still might get it wrong, even if you're Giovanni De Rocco. When he isn't happy with a flavor (it must be perfect), he throws it out. To him, it's either good or not good. There's no in-between.

He is very fussy about all of his ingredients—organic lemons from Sorrento, the finest quality eggs from a supplier in Padova that the family has used for 70 years, and vanilla from Madagascar. The aroma is incredible.

Vanilla connoisseurs say Madagascar produces the most distinctive and flavorful vanilla in the world. For that reason, and the fact that it harvests a yearly crop of 120 million vanilla beans, it's sometimes called the vanilla island. The spice originated in Mexico, where the Spanish conquistadors stole vanilla pods from the Aztecs and took them overseas. They were eventually replanted on the French Reunion Island (the former Bourbon Island) near Madagascar and from there spread to Indonesia, the Comoros, Tahiti, and Tonga.

Gelateria Alpina sits on the ground floor of a building constructed in 1848. To see the original and much lower level of the street, go to nearby Fortezza da Basso, which was built in the record time of one year—1534–1535. Supposedly the fortress was to protect Florence from invasion, but it often became a political refuge for the Medici during times of civil unrest. This explains why the strongest side faces toward the city.

Architect Antonio da Sangallo, who received the commission from Alessandro de' Medici, designed the pentagon-shaped fort so that it was almost impregnable and could be defended by a minimum of men. Throughout its long history, it has never been attacked, except by present-day exhibitors and trade-fair visitors. It's now used as the main exhibit center for Florence and houses high-profile events such as the Florence Gift Mart, Pitti Immagine Uomo (men's fashion), Il Salone del Mobile (furniture) and La Mostra Internationale dell'Artigianato (handcrafts).

Fortezza da Basso and Alpina are both located on Via Filippo Strozzi. It's not clear which Filippo Strozzi is the street's namesake. There were many.

The Strozzi family, wealthy Florentine nobles, formed an alliance with the

Albizzi, who were rivals of the powerful Medici. Consequently, in 1434, the Strozzi were exiled (it was not a good idea to make enemies of the Medici). The family soon recovered, however, and headed south to become bankers for the King of Naples.

Filippo Strozzi returned to Florence in 1466 flush with florins and decided to show off by building the largest palazzo in the city. To do this, he acquired a dozen or so different buildings and demolished them. The result of his efforts was Palazzo Strozzi—the most opulent palazzo built during the zenith of Florence in the 1400s. When Filippo I died in 1491, his son Filippo II continued with the project, until he led an uprising against the ruthless Cosimo I de' Medici. (Big mistake.) Filippo was thrown in prison, where he committed suicide. Yet another Filippo Strozzi fought for the French against the Spanish and was killed in a naval battle near the Azores in 1582. Palazzo Strozzi eventually bankrupted the family.

Around this period of history—the mid-1500s—Buontalenti and Ruggeri developed Italian gelato as we know it. (See the section on Badiani for more about them.) Folklore tells us, though, that gelato in various forms existed long before these two men.

According to the Bible, Abraham tasted gelato's distant cousin when Isaac offered him goat's milk mixed with snow.

In ancient Egypt, snow was stored in insulated buildings throughout the summer, allowing pharaohs to offer their guests the ancient equivalent of a snow cone: fruit juice and snow served in silver goblets.

Alexander the Great ate honey and fruit mixed with snow to give him energy during his march to India.

Roman general Quinto Fabio Massimo created the first formal recipe for faux gelato made with snow from Etna and Vesuvius.

A disciple of Mohammed discovered a way to freeze fruit juice in a container and then place it in another container formed out of chopped ice, thus increasing longevity. Eventually, the Arabs added sugar to this frozen fruit juice concoction to create sorbet, which was introduced to Europe through Sicily.

Though tracing the exact evolution of gelato is difficult, it clearly traveled a path from east to west, where the Italians, with their flair and creativity, made this frozen delight what it is today.

Half the Alpina clients are Fiorentini and the other half tourists—and it never feels crowded. After May 1, sit outside and enjoy your gelato. Inside you'll find a light and airy bar area, which was at one time living quarters for owner Giovanni De Rocco's great uncle. Matteo, De Rocco's son, makes an excellent espresso. In Florence they say, "You need three things for good caffé. It has to be pagato, caldo, *and* berlo seduto." *Paid for, hot, and enjoyed while sitting.*

Marzocco

Via Cernaia 16/r
055 470581
Open 7AM—8PM
Closed 12PM—2PM, Saturday & Sunday only
Open daily

*W*arning: Visiting Marzocco may turn you into a chocoholic.

Small and narrow with a stand-up bar, cioccolateria-pasticceria Marzocco is one of those neighborhood places you probably wouldn't give a second look. But, as they say in Italy: *Non giudicare un libro dalla sua copertina*. (Don't judge a book by its cover.)

Downstairs in the *laboratorio*, owner Alessandro Stocchi, along with wife Clarissa and seven employees, makes the incredible Marzocco chocolates sold from glass displays in the front of the shop.

"Originally, this was a coal depot," says Stocchi. "About 60 years ago in the garden out the back, they sold coal to the locals. At some point, the owner of the building closed the depot, put in an oven, and began selling pastries. My father bought the pasticceria in 1960—he died in 1998."

When the elder Stocchi took over the business, it was already called Marzocco—the name refers to the emblem of Florence, a seated lion whose right paw rests on a shield emblazoned with an iris. The lion symbolizes strength and the iris, freedom.

Chocolate was not the first thing on the family's mind in those early days—it was pastry. "I started making pastry in the *laboratorio* at eighteen. My father worked only in the bar," Stocchi says. Over the years, he built up a reputation as a first rate *pasticciere* (pastry maker), yet he wanted to do something that would truly set Marzocco apart. In 1985, Alessandro Stocchi decided to make *cioccolato artigianale* (handmade chocolate).

"I started working with chocolate as a passion," he says. Twenty years ago, most Italians did not seem to share this passion. They would buy a nice box of chocolates occasionally as a gift for someone special, but there was no culture of eating chocolate for pleasure as in France, Belgium, and Switzerland. Little by little, things changed—chocolate consumption in Italy has increased from an average of half a kilo per person a year in the mid-80s to almost 3 kilos per person in 2003.

This is as good a place as any for History of Chocolate 101.

Some say the cocoa plant originated 4,000 years ago in the Orinoco Valley of Venezuela; others claim it was the Amazon Basin of Brazil. In AD 600, the Mayas brought the plant with them to the Yucatan and established cocoa tree plantations. Eventually the Aztecs subjugated the Mayas (around AD 1200), collecting tribute in the form of cocoa beans.

Both Mayas and Aztecs made a chocolate drink by roasting beans and grinding them to paste, which they then dissolved in water. The Aztecs called it *cacahautl*. This is the very drink that Montezuma, the powerful Aztec emperor of Mexico (and major chocoholic), consumed in great quantities—50 or more goblets of chocolate per day. His preferred style: honey-thick, flavored with vanilla and spices, and served cold. Montezuma often drank chocolate before entering his harem, which caused the Spaniards to think that this drink put lead in the pencil.

The brutal explorer Hernando Cortez didn't much care for the bitter flavor; in 1528, however, he brought three chests of cocoa beans back to the court of King Charles V of Spain as a gift. Cortez noticed the Aztecs used beans as currency and came up with the idea to start cocoa plantations on Trinidad and Haiti, growing "money" to trade for Aztec gold.

As a result, Spain monopolized the cocoa trade for almost 100 years, and in the bargain, kept the chocolate formula secret. During this time, the nobility—the only ones enjoying the drink—invented hot chocolate as we know it today by adding cane sugar and heating the concoction.

It was Spanish monks, consigned to process the cocoa into chocolate, who eventually let the secret out in 1606. Soon after, Italian traveler Antonio Carletti blabbed it around Europe. By 1657, the first of the famous English chocolate houses (competing with coffee houses) opened in London. The beverage was still very expensive, though—a drink only for the elite.

By 1730, the steam engine mechanized the cocoa grinding process, lowering the price from about $3 a pound to a figure within almost everyone's reach.

The next milestone in the history of chocolate was the creation

of cocoa powder in 1828 by a Dutch chemist named Conrad J. van Houten. He patented an inexpensive method for pressing the fat (cocoa butter) from roasted and ground cocoa beans (called chocolate liquor in the biz) using a hydraulic press. The leftover cocoa cake he then ground into a fine powder and treated with alkaline salts so it mixed easily with water. In addition to giving the beverage a smoother consistency and improved flavor, cocoa powder reduced prices even further.

Twenty years later, chocolate moved from the realm of drink to that of candy when van Houten made the first solid eating chocolate by mixing sugar and cocoa butter with the chocolate liquor.

Then in 1879, Swiss candy maker Daniel Peter found a way to add powdered milk to chocolate creating the first—you guessed it—milk chocolate. (For Making of Chocolate 101, see the Hemingway chapter.)

According to Alessandro Stocchi, however, milk chocolate is at the bottom of the chocolate pecking order. "That type of chocolate leaves a sweet, cloying aftertaste. Your tongue feels coated. The more bitter the chocolate, the cleaner your mouth feels after you've eaten it.

"When a person comes here for the first time, I try to get them to taste the more bitter chocolate… to coax them into it… guide them to the really good chocolate.

"Someone who only likes sweet chocolate…we give them bitter chocolate by small gradations. Eventually they'll taste the difference and won't eat the sweet chocolate any more. Sweet chocolate is like eating a spoonful of sugar.

"We make chocolate candy that's 56 percent cocoa, another that's 76 percent and finally one that's much more bitter than the others—90 percent for those people who want the maximum chocolate flavor."

From time to time, Stocchi hosts a chocolate tasting (much like a wine tasting), which takes his guests on a culinary journey from sweet to bitter. "Between tastes, we cleanse the palate with a piece of bread so it's ready for the next flavor. Little by little, they taste the difference… from less sugar to more cocoa… until we arrive at the best chocolate. They always leave appreciating *cioccolato amaro* (bitter chocolate)," says Stocchi.

In addition to being a candy maker, Stocchi is a sculptor—he copies Michelangelo's David and Botticelli's Venus in white chocolate with an attention to detail that's incredible. The process takes about three days: First, he creates a plaster form; then, he makes a silicon mold; and finally, he pours the chocolate. After it sets, he removes little imperfections by hand.

He also makes smoking pipes and tools—including a hammer, pliers, nuts and bolts, and a toolbox—all from dark chocolate. He's so skilled that when a bricklayer client specially ordered a *cazzuola* (trowel) as a gift, Stocchi says, "I put my chocolate trowel next to the real one and he couldn't tell the difference."

If Alessandro Stocchi is in the laboratorio *(located at the back of the bar, down half a flight of stairs), ask him to come up and give you his chocolate taste test—a journey from cloying sweet to refreshing bitter. Every one of his chocolates has a distinct flavor: Try the* sospiri al rhum, tartufo al caffé, prugna e armanac, *or the spicy* tequila e peperoncino. *Remember, his chocolates go well with his excellent coffee. If you're inclined to feel guilty about eating chocolate, a recent study by the University of Glasgow and Italy's National Institute for Food and Nutrition Research says that dark chocolate (in moderation) can raise blood antioxidant levels by 20 percent.*

Perché No!

Via dei Tavolini, 19/r
055 2398969
Open noon—11PM, Wednesday to
Monday in winter
11AM—midnight, Wednesday to
Monday in summer
Closed Tuesdays

You may have heard of I Califfi (The Califfs), a Florence-based, progressive-rock band that released eleven singles and two albums in the late-'60s and early-'70s. And then again, maybe you haven't. Ciro Cammilli, owner of Perché No! gelateria, plays guitar with the latest incarnation of the group led by two original members, keyboard player Giacomo Romoli and singer Marcovecchio.

You could say that Cammilli's day job is making fine *gelato artigianale*, which he has done since he bought the gelateria in 1991. "I got married young and worked 20 years in my own business… a *pelletteria*." says Cammilli. "We were leather artisans making purses for important brands like Prada and Gucci. Then I had a chance to buy this business. From the time I was a boy working in a gelateria during the summer, I was always interested in gelato."

The original owner of Perché No!, Ugo Ravaioli, first came up with the idea for the business in the fall of 1938. He noticed a neglected shop run by an old Swiss gentleman who sold polenta and chestnut cake, and said to himself—you guessed it—"*Perché no!*" (Why not!) The location on Via dei Tavolini—just around the corner from Piazza della Signoria—was the perfect spot for a gelateria. Ravaioli purchased the business, and in early 1939, with renovations completed, he began selling his homemade gelato. When the outbreak of World War II interrupted the supply of fresh milk and cream, Ravaioli and his wife Maria improvised—creating their own spumoni with egg whites and a cream made from apples.

After the Allies took Florence in 1944, a group of American soldiers came to Perché No! looking for its famous gelato. Of course, there wasn't any—by this time, Ravaioli had no ingredients and no electrical power. The soldiers were disappointed, but not deterred. They offered to supply powdered milk, eggs, sugar, and gelatin, along with an electric generator if Ravaioli would come to their camp to make gelato. For some reason he was not comfortable with this arrangement—so they brought the ingredients to him as well as restoring power to his shop. In the bargain, electricity was restored to half of Via dei Tavolini. The Americans got their gelato, and Ravaioli's neighbors were the first in Florence to turn on the lights after the Germans left town.

Perché No! was run by Ravaioli family members until 1986 when the employees took over. During the next five years, things went downhill quickly. "We took over in 1991," says Cammilli. "The shop was dirty and the gelato was not what it should have been. An older woman… part of the original family… worked with us for a couple years after we bought it. She wanted us to continue the tradition of making old-fashioned gelato, the way they had since 1939, and we were happy to do it."

Many of the gelaterias in the *centro storico* are aimed exclusively at the tourist who stops once, never to return. Cammilli claims that the gelaterias on Via dei Calzaiuoli, the main street near Perché No! are for the most part *industriale*. The makers of *gelato artigianale* refer to gelato made with a pre-made base of eggs, milk, and sugar along with powdered flavoring as *gelato industriale*.

"Today, all you need is a telephone, a location, a gelato machine, and a supplier—in three days you can be in business making gelato. But what kind of gelato? Our type of gelato? No!

"In the *centro*, gelato also costs more because rents are higher. They raise the rents all the time. A clothing store on the corner that had been here for a long time just closed—they were paying 2,200 euros. The next tenant paid 11,000 euros.

"You can taste the difference between the tourist places and Perché No! Every once in a while a tourist passes by—often an American mother—with an ice cream in one hand and a small child without ice cream in the other. The baby wants its own gelato, so the mother stops in and buys a cone for the little one. Outside, the mother tastes the

baby's cone, then throws hers away, and eats the baby's—because the mother had been eating industrial ice cream."

Cammilli often comes up against a public more concerned with appearance than substance. This happened recently with his strawberry gelato; the fresh strawberries at the market were light in color, and consequently the strawberry gelato was a pale pink. A customer saw this and thought maybe there was a problem. "I could artificially color the gelato, but this is absurd. The most important thing is the flavor. The fruit is different every time you buy it, so tomorrow the gelato is going to look different than today," he says.

Cammilli is a member of the Slow Food movement—no surprise since he makes his gelato very slowly and carefully.

This movement started back in 1986, when MacDonald's invaded the eternal city and set up its golden arches next to the Spanish Steps. Italian journalist Carlo Petrini was outraged (as well he should have been), so in reaction, he created Slow Food—an organization dedicated to saving regional products and cuisines of the world from the industrial food culture. Its symbol is the snail: small, slow, and prudent—everything that goes against the modern world's obsession with speed.

The Slow Food movement even has its own manifesto. It states, in part:

> ...Against those who confuse efficiency with frenzy... against the homogeneity of Fast Food, we rediscover the richness and the aroma of local cuisines. If Fast

Food, in the name of productivity, has modified our life and threatened the environment and landscape, Slow Food is today the answer of the vanguard."

Slow Food focuses on things such as saving a rare peach or preserving a special type of prosciutto. An example of the latter happened recently in the small town of Zibello, known for its *culatello*, which comes from the muscles of a pig's back legs. Aficionados say that the flavor of Culatello di Zibello blows Prosciutto di Parma out of the water—yet its production was dying out. Inspired by the Slow Food movement, Zibello organized the Festivale del Culatello, dedicated to showcasing the tender ham. The annual four-day event, attracting thousands of people, has publicized this delicacy—and saved it from extinction. Since its inception, Slow Food has spread worldwide with 70,000 members in 42 countries.

The recent Slow Cities movement is a spin-off of Slow Food. The idea: to make Italian cities under 50,000 people more livable by banning traffic from the *centro*, improving parks, and limiting fast food places to the *periferia* (periphery). It's an effort to preserve the long lunch, the early-evening *passeggiata* (leisurely stroll), and shopping on the main piazzas. In a nutshell, Slow Cities draws a line in the sand and says, "Enough with the creeping sameness, and 24/7-how-fast-can-I-go-how-many-things-can-I-accomplish speed of modern lives."

When you stop by Perché No!, you'll most likely be served by either Ciro Cammilli, his wife Paola, or one of their two daughters, Cecilia and Valentina. Sometimes it's crowded (only because the gelato is great) so you may have to be patient. If you're a clock-watcher, check out the onyx wall clock created by a Florentine mosaic artist Giovanni Fiaschi in 1950. Gelato recommendations: the pistacchio *may be the best in the world;* crema *is great; and during the summer, go for one of the fruit flavors (made only with sugar, fruit, and water). The lemon tastes like a real lemon.*

Vivoli

Via Isola delle Stinche, 7/r
055 292334
Open 7:30AM—1AM, Tuesday to Saturday
9:30AM—1AM, Sunday
Closed Mondays

Shortly after being interviewed for this book, Piero Vivoli, "*Il babbo del gelato*" (the father of gelato), as the Florence daily newspaper *La Nazione* called him, died suddenly of a heart attack. This chapter is dedicated to Piero.

Piero Vivoli was the poet of gelato. To hear him read the copy he wrote for his brochure, in his deep sonorous voice, was like listening to Dylan Thomas recite one of his poems.

Il piacere di fare gelato,
il piacere di assaggiarlo,
il piacere di offrirlo…
il nostro gelato e' fatto
con ottime materie prime,
professionalita e amore…

Which simply translates to the following:

The pleasure of making gelato
the pleasure of tasting it
the pleasure of offering it…
our gelato is made
with the best ingredients,
professionalism and love…

Piero was very proud of the gelato he produced. And, fortunately for all of us, the tradition continues with his wife Simonetta and two daughters—Silvana, the gelato maker, and Patrizia, the administrator.

In 1929, Piero's father, Raffaello Vivoli, moved to Florence from the country where times were hard; somehow he managed to start a *latteria* (milk bar). Soon it expanded, selling *panna* (cream) and eventually gelato, which became its cash cow and claim to fame.

"There was no refrigerator in those days. Our first counter used ice to keep the gelato cold. When I was 4 or 5 I would break up the ice and bring it to my father in a bucket. I helped him like my children help me," explained Piero.

Piero grew up in the gelateria and over the years developed a feeling for the pulse of Vivoli. When he came to work each morning, he'd stop in the doorway for four or five seconds, look around, and "taste the day" as he put it. "The nose, the mouth, the eyes… give you a sensation of the state of the business… as if it were a person. The one behind the espresso machine has been with us 15 or 20 years. We look at each other. I notice if there is a smile or a question. That is how my day begins."

Piero referred to the business as a *bottega* (shop) because this word evokes more than just a place to work for the 23 employees. It suggests creativity and a sense of quality. For many years he stood behind the counter, serving customers, and observing them. Not surprisingly, he was full of stories about his customers.

Everyday at noon, five "college girls," obviously tourists, came into Vivoli and ordered five large gelatos. Finally after a week, Piero asked how much longer they were going to visit Florence. The answer: "Three more gelatos." They were measuring their time not in days, but in Vivoli gelato.

Many people began as clients and became friends. One Sunday, a long-time client (and old friend) came in and told Piero, "I had a bad day, but I knew that if I went to Vivoli I'd feel better." Piero especially liked this incident because he always said, "I'm offering people well being. Something that will make them feel better, not worse. When a person enters Vivoli, it's someone who has faith in that, and in the business."

Another time, a middle-aged blonde woman ordered gelato and Piero remembered her face. He said, "We've met before." She said, "Yes… 25 years ago. How is the gelato?" Piero answered, "Like always." A couple bites of gelato later, she smiled and agreed.

One of Piero's biggest challenges came when he was asked to make a *torta di gelato* (ice cream cake) for the birthday of Giovanni Spadolini—university professor, historian, and well-known Italian politician. (A genuine *pezzo grosso*, or big shot.) Spadolini's sister-in-law ordered the cake a month ahead of time, and for the entire month Piero was uninspired. "I feel like an artist when I make gelato. Instead of a canvas and paints, I have ingredients. I had to say something with this gelato."

Twenty-four hours before the event, still nothing. "I was becoming nervous… bad tempered. Nothing was working. Suddenly it came to me. In a big wooden tray, I made the symbol of the Spadolini's political party in green and red gelato. On top of that I created a rolled-up chocolate parchment and wrote some elegant good wishes." Spadolini was so pleased that he sent Piero an autographed copy of his latest book.

Piero also officially qualified as an FOB (Friend of Bill). During one of Clinton's presidential visits to Italy, a member of his entourage familiar with Vivoli had a couple kilos of the gelateria's best sent to Air Force One for the long flight home.

Piero's daughter Silvana, the current gelato maker, also has a story about a command performance for Dustin Hoffman. The actor flew her to L.A. to make the famous Vivoli gelato for his special 12-person dinner at a Brentwood restaurant. Word spread through the Hollywood network of gelato lovers—one of them being *pezzo grosso* Michael Eisner who was informed of Silvana's arrival with the words, "The queen has arrived."

When a few Tuscan gelato makers formed a group in 1960 to raise the awareness of *gelato artigianale* (homemade gelato)—giving the occupation of gelato maker standards and status—Piero Vivoli was among them. He often spoke with passion about the artisan.

"What is an *artigiano*? It's a person that works with their hands, their experience, their sensitivities... with their *forza d'anima* (force of their soul). They create with everything that is inside of them. The individual expression of the *artigiano* transmits itself through the work," says Piero.

"I have always said to my daughters. You need plans and dreams. You have to be thinking about what you are doing, and you need time. I am always thinking, dreaming about things to do.

"In the end, a smile is worth more than money. The greatest payment is a smile from someone you've pleased with your creation."

You should smile, too—when you look across the street at Teatro Verdi, with a cup of luscious gelato in your hand, and appreciate the fact that you're not in the horrible

Stinche prison, which stood in that same spot until 1838 when it was torn down. Teatro Verdi, constructed in 1854, is the home of the Orchestra della Toscana, not to mention one of Italy's largest theaters and a venue for ballet, opera, pop and jazz concerts, and film previews.

The Vivoli address—Via Isola delle Stinche—refers to the fact that Stinche prison was technically an island surrounded by a large moat. The name itself comes from the rebellious Stinche castle located outside of the city. In 1304, the Signoria (Florence's ruling council) captured some of the Stinche soldiers and locked them away in a specially constructed prison. Originally limited to prisoners of war and political prisoners, in the 1400s the prison population was expanded to include thieves, murderers, prostitutes, debtors, and the bankrupt (no bankruptcy-law protection in those days). They were all mixed in together, with an occasional big name like Machiavelli or Giovanni Cavalcante, a composer who had the bad judgment to write an unflattering opera about the exile of Cosimo I. Cold, cunning Cosimo was the least loved of the Medici.

What were conditions like in Stinche prison? Not good: there were high walls, no windows, and mean guards. You paid the outrageous sum of one florin a day for a straw sleeping mat and dreadful rations. If you didn't pay, you didn't eat—and worse. Torture was common, including the removal of eyes, ears, and limbs.

But according to John Howard, who wrote a book in the 1780s with the catchy title, *The State of Prisons in England and Wales with preliminary Observations and an Account of some foreign Prisons and Hospital*, conditions eventually improved.

> …there are five doors to pass before you come to the court. The opening of the first is three feet wide, and four feet nine inches high, with an inscription over it Oportet Misereri (We ought to be compassionate.) In this prison were forty-two men and fourteen women. Debtors were not separated from criminals. In one room were eight who paid for their beds. The bread was good: the daily allowance to each, fifteen ounces. None were in irons.

Vivoli is among the most well-known and popular gelaterias in Florence. Don't let a long line put you off. Vivoli has rush periods all day and they can occur anytime. Service is fast, so if it's crowded when you arrive, wait until the smoke clears, and step up to the counter. Not sure which flavor to choose? They're happy to give you a taste. For something different, try zabaglione *(a mixture of eggs and* vino marsala*). Another winner: silky rich chocolate-orange gelato.*

· 2 ·

OLTRARNO

It means "the other side of the Arno" and refers generally to the area across the river from the centro storico. We've chosen two places: one on the well-known Piazzale Michelangelo, and the other in the hip Borgo San Frediano area, with its artisan studios, cheaper trattorias, and fewer tourists.

Hemingway

Piazza Piattellina 9/r
055 284781
Open 4:30PM—1AM, Tuesday to Thursday
4:30PM—2AM, Friday & Saturday
11AM—8PM, Sunday
Closed Mondays

*H*uge black and white prints of "Papa" adorn the walls as you enter the café— he looms large, as he did in the literary world during the 1920s and '30s.

Owner Emma Mantovani says she and partner Giovanna Bagni named the business after the writer because of his *vita artistica e errabonda* (artistic, vagabond life)—he resided in France, Italy, Spain, Cuba, Idaho, and Key West; and hunted in Africa. This international approach is reflected in the fine menu, an eclectic draw of recipes from around the world. But the real star of Hemingway is the chocolate—especially designer chocolate pastries made by *cioccolatieri* such as Paul De Bondt, Andrea Slitti, and Luca Mannori.

Let's talk chocolate for a minute. You probably take it for granted because you don't realize how much is involved in producing chocolate—even for a simple candy bar.

We start with the cocoa beans, which are actually seeds living inside a pod about the size of a pineapple that hangs from a cocoa tree. The seeds are removed from ripe pods and dried for about a week before being shipped to the chocolate maker.

Once the chocolate maker gets the beans, he blends and roasts them—followed by winnowing, or removing the brittle shell from the nib (meat). The nibs are ground, and because they're half fat, they form a viscous liquid called chocolate liquor. When the liquor is poured into a mold and allowed to solidify, it becomes unsweetened chocolate.

You also can put the chocolate liquor into a hydraulic press and squeeze out the fat. The leftover pressed cake becomes cocoa powder; the fat or cocoa butter is used to make both white chocolate and brown chocolate. (For History of Chocolate 101, see the Marzocco listing.)

Price varies depending on the processing and the quality of the original ingredients. The better chocolate is made with high-quality cocoa beans and a greater percentage of cocoa butter. "We use only *cioccolato di prima qualità*," says Emma. "We buy it in small lots—maybe 5 kilos—and use it to make our hot chocolate. We never use anything powdered or pre-made."

Strangely enough, Hemingway grew out of an Indian cooking school that Emma Mantovani started with two partners in 1989. They chose Indian-style cooking because there were already many Italian cooking schools in Florence, and they wanted to do something different. "It was difficult at first because we couldn't find any Indian cookbooks, and ingredients were not common. London was the closest place that had anything. But, eventually the school was a success," says Emma.

The partners became interested in chocolate when they attended the first Festival Eurochocolate Perugia (an international chocolate show) in 1993 and rubbed elbows with the best chocolate makers on the planet. As a result, they

decided to push their culinary envelope in the direction of a chocolate bar and café—and opened Hemingway in October of 1996.

For a location, they chose a former *alimentari* (grocery store) in a 15th-century building in San Frediano, one of the oldest areas in Firenze. A third partner in the venture had experience with restoration, so she acted as project manager (she has since left the business). The group completely transformed the interior, scrubbing away centuries of paint and dirt from all the surfaces and removing columns to open up the space.

"To begin here in San Frediano was not easy," says Emma "There's not as much tourist traffic as in the *centro* and around the Duomo. It's not as well known, but we thought it was a beautiful zone… very typical Fiorentino… and it's still that way. At this point, we've reached our goal of becoming known for *cioccolato artigianale*. It's the specialty of the house, especially our *cioccolata calda* (hot chocolate). Plus we've brought our international cooking background to bear on the menu.

"I worked in a bank at the same time I did the cooking school and I'm glad to be out of banking. This is something completely different. It's very enjoyable to see people's immediate reaction. And I like talking to customers. The clientele is mixed—we want it that way. We get lots of foreigners, along with Italians that come from outside the *comune* of Florence—from Pistoia or Pisa."

One of the foreigners you would have noticed in Hemingway a few years ago is the English actor Daniel Day-Lewis, famous for roles in films such as *My Beautiful Laundrette*, Martin Scorcese's version of Edith Wharton's *The Age of Innocence*, and most recently, *Gangs of New York*. In need of a sabbatical, Day-Lewis—legendary for his intensity both on and off the screen—took five years off starting in 1997. Most of 1999 he spent in Florence with his wife Rebecca Miller, daughter of playwright Arthur Miller, and the couple's son. During that time, Day–Lewis became enamored of the shoemaking business and apprenticed himself to master shoemaker Stefano Bemer.

"He became one of our regulars when he was living here," says Emma Mantovani. "We saw him often in the evenings. The first time he came in, people noticed him—he is a nice-looking man. And then, they kept staring because they recognized him, and wondered what a well-known actor like him was doing in San Frediano. But he kept to himself—he is shy and reserved and didn't want to cause a stir. He always took a table in a corner or a seat at the bar behind a column. No one ever approached him or talked to him. They left him alone."

As a visitor to Hemingway, you would also be walking in the footsteps of Italian film director Lina Wertmuller, who got her start with Fellini. The café hosted a special evening for the controversial Wertmuller in 2002. She's best known for her collaborations with actor Giancarlo Gianinni in such films as *Love and Anarchy*, *Swept Away*, and *The Seven Beauties*.

On your way to or from Hemingway, make it a priority to pass through Porta San Frediano, the city gate located off Via Pisana. It was built in 1324 as part of the third medieval wall. Each time Florence expanded outside of its existing walls—in the form of *borghi* (little villages or suburbs)—the city would eventually have to build a new larger enclosure to protect itself from arch-rivals such as Pisa. This happened three times between 1078 and 1333 when the third medieval wall was completed. During the 1200s, the city's population doubled—from 50,000 to 100,000—and it reached a size and shape that would remain constant until the 1800s.

Porta San Frediano is a magnificent portal—huge old wooden doors covered with giant metal studs. You can almost see the guards pulling them open in the morning and creaking them closed at night. Above the arch on the inside, look for the Florentine coat of arms, and on the outside of the doors you'll find large metal rings—the ideal place to tie your horse.

Right near Hemingway on Piazza del Carmine sits the church Santa Maria del Carmine, worth visiting for the Brancacci Chapel. In addition to the bones of the wealthy Brancacci family, the chapel contains frescoes by Masolino, Masaccio, and Filippino Lippi considered the zenith of this Renaissance art form. The chapel is dedicated to the Virgin Mary, who must have been protecting it (and the marvelous frescoes) when a devastating 1771 fire destroyed most of the church, but left the chapel intact.

After you're frescoed out, it's good to know that Hemingway is literally two minutes away on foot.

Wicker chairs, soft colors, pictures of a happy "Papa" Hemingway—they all work together to create a relaxing atmosphere and a contemporary feel in a very old space. A must try: the hot chocolate with a touch of red pepper. Sunday brunch (served 11:30—2:30 from October to May) is good, too—with typical American dishes, including apple pie. Tea lovers can choose from a selection of Les Contes de Thé di Parigi, and every cup of excellent cappuccino comes with a chocolate spoon that disappears slowly as you stir.

Ristorante Michelangelo

**Viale Galileo Galilei, 2/r
(Piazzale Michelangelo)
055 2342705
Open 6:30AM–3:30AM, daily**
*Closed Wednesdays from
November to February*

At a tourist destination such as Piazzale Michelangelo you'd expect to find a tourist trap that sells mediocre food and industrial gelato to busloads of one-time visitors. That's definitely not the case.

"It's always a surprise that you eat well here," says owner Marco Vignolini. "Afterward, visitors talk about the place and we get good word-of-mouth. Whoever comes to Florence, comes to Piazzale Michelangelo. This is automatic. And because they come to us, there's lots of opportunities. When I took this place over, the Fiorentini didn't come here. Now they do—and every time, it gets better; we get more and more organized. But we're not where we want to be, yet."

In a relatively short period of time, Vignolini has brought Michelangelo from a fading venue to a flourishing multifaceted *locale* (business), which includes an indoor restaurant, a casual terrace dining area, a gelateria (he makes his own gelato from scratch), and an American-style bar. And he has big plans, or *grossi programmi* as he says, to build a patio in the back for the warm summer evenings, plus expand the menu, and offer more live music. But then Marco Vignolini is the kind of man who always has big plans. He is the epitome of an entrepreneur, always with the big picture in mind. (Put

him in Silicon Valley in the 1990s, and he'd have been right at home.)

"I can't stay in the *laboratorio* making gelato, or behind the stove in the kitchen," he explains. "I'm always thinking, creating, organizing—moving things ahead. *Ci vuole la fantasia* (you need imagination)."

Vignolini's restlessness took him overseas. "In the beginning, I was fine in Florence. Then I decided I wanted to immigrate. Go somewhere that's hot in the winter." So, he did. He went to Rio and opened a nightclub. Although a bit mysterious about how things went, he says that Brazil is not the land of opportunity and he wouldn't go there again to invest. "Make your money at home," he says. "The place you know best. And spend it overseas." Living three months of the year in Brazil on the ocean would be ideal for him. Apparently, Brazilians who live inland differ from the coastal dwellers. "The people of Sao Paolo say they applaud anyone from Rio who works. They never work in Rio. They never work by the sea. They just enjoy themselves," says Vignolini.

When you stop by Michelangelo to enjoy an espresso or cappuccino, you'll see a huge, antique coffee machine (the size of R2-D2 in the *Star Wars* movies) made by Arduino, one of the original espresso machine makers.

It took a long time for the coffee maker to evolve to its present state. In the mid-1700s, the *bollitore di Baghdad* (Baghdad kettle) arrived from the Middle East. It had a cover, a bulbous base with a flame underneath, and a curved handle—an Arabian nights coffeepot. You boiled the roasted coffee beans in the water to make the brew.

The infusion method came next—the great-great-great-grand-father of today's filtered coffee. Ground coffee went into a linen sack, which was placed in a pot of boiling water.

Before going any further, you should know your Italian coffee-pot vocabulary. Technically, *la caffettiera* is a container for serving coffee, not making coffee. *La caffettiera a filtro* (with a filter) falls in the gray area—the water is boiled elsewhere, then coffee is made and served in the caffettiera. *La macchina per il caffè* (coffee machine) handles the entire cycle from boiling the water to producing the liquid itself.

During the 1800s, engineers, silversmiths, tinsmiths, and housewives

tried to design the perfect coffee machine—using steam, thermodynamics, vacuums, and hydrostatics. A Mr. Jones from London invented a pump and percolation machine in 1819, as did a French woman named Richard in 1837. In about 1819, a Frenchman came up with a coffeemaker that performed its task directly at the table.

French, German, Austrian, and English coffee fanatics developed variations of steam technology that pushed brewed coffee directly into a cup. And in 1833, a Londoner filed a patent for a machine that forced water up through the filter, spouting coffee toward the glass dome, which cascaded down like a Trevi fountain of espresso.

The French also experimented with using a vacuum to pull water from one cylinder, through a connecting filter with ground coffee, into a second cylinder. Another machine automatically turned off its flame when the coffee was made.

By the late 1800s, only the wealthy or upper middle class could purchase any of these high-tech machines. Most people boiled water in a pot or pan and added a little coffee. From 1900–1930, companies such as Eterna, Pavoni, Simerac, Neowatt, and Victoria Arduino sold elegant brass and nickel-plaited, electric machines. Then, in 1933, life became a lot easier for the average Italian coffee lover when Bialetti marketed its first "Napoletana," the aluminum, stovetop coffee maker still used today.

The next evolution came shortly after World War II, when Gaggia manufactured *il sistema a pistone*, which forced boiling water, instead of steam, through the coffee with a piston activated by a hand lever. (Steam tended to burn the coffee.) Today, many claim that these hand-operated machines produce the best espresso with the richest *crema* (head), and Vignolini is one of them.

Pier Teresio Arduino started his company in 1905, naming it Victoria Arduino after his wife. The handcrafted bronze eagle on the top of Vignolini's Arduino along with the vertical *caldaia* (boiler), designed that way for both functional and aesthetic reasons, makes the older machine very distinctive.

This lovely old coffee-maker lives at the bar on the terrace, managed by Ahmid, a movie-star handsome Egyptian in his early 30s. Ahmid came to Italy to escape the Egyptian military service. After the age of 30, you can return, pay a $2,000 fine, and all is forgiven (which he did). But at this point, Ahmid says he is more Italian than Egyptian.

Another key employee, Fulvia, Marco Vignolini's extremely competent right-hand person and an attractive middle-aged woman, started with the entrepreneur when she was 18 and has worked with him continuously through all of his enterprises. "I worked for him before he went to Brazil and afterward when he had a business that made metal fittings—there were a hundred employees. And then there was another one with 30 people. He also had a couple of discotheques here in Florence before this place," she says.

She is the go-to person. "If something isn't working, and he's not here, they come to me. I do everything… the scheduling… the bookkeeping… I work a long day. I was lucky enough to have my mother-in-law live with me and my husband, and look after the children while I worked," she continues. "Now they're grown up. I'm hardly ever home these days. I'm always here. It is very demanding and exacting work."

Giuseppe Poggi, another hardworking Fiorentino, created Piazzale Michelangelo when Florence became capital of the Kingdom of Italy from 1865 to 1871 (see the section on Caffé Gilli). Poggi's controversial plan for the needed urban expansion included tearing down sections of the medieval walls to make way for winding avenues around the outer edge of the city, which gave Florence an attractive, livable exterior, different from that of most large Italian cities, with their tidy *centro storicos* surrounded by bleak industrial belts.

Poggi laid out Piazzale Michelangelo in 1869, naming it after the great artistic genius; a copy of his David stands there. It was not a success at first, even though it provided the first truly romantic panorama of Florence. The Fiorentini of the day were wrong, though; Poggi was right. Tourists mob this famous view, which is definitely worth a visit.

Walk to Piazzale Michelangelo. It's not far—take Ponte alle Grazie to Via San Niccolò to Via del Monte alle Croci then up the steps on Via di San Salvatore al Monte. Once there, go to Ristorante Michelangelo. You'll eat with locals, politicians, and celebrities such as cantautore *(singer/songwriter) Renato Zero and well-known Italian actor and screenwriter Paolo Villaggio. Order a salad, ravioli, and* salsiccia e fagioli *(grilled sausage and Tuscan beans). Afterwards try a glass of moscato and Michelangelo's cheese plate (the* pecorino saltato *is unique). But wait, there's more: the* crema di paradiso *(creme caramel) paired with a glass of* fragolino *(light, fizzy, strawberry-flavored dessert wine). Then roll back down the hill.*

· 3 ·

LE CURE

This area in the northeast side of the city—a short bus ride or a long walk from the centro storico *—was developed in the 1920s and early 1930s. The first thing you'll notice about its pleasant, upper-middle-class neighborhoods is that there are no tourists. We chose two places on either end of Via dei Mille: one on Piazza delle Cure and the other closer to Campo di Marte.*

Badiani

Viale dei Mille, 20/r
055 578682
Open 7AM—1AM
7AM—midnight, Sunday
Closed Tuesdays

*T*here are three good reasons to visit Badiani: extraordinary pastries and gelato, great coffee, and the owner Orazio Pomposi—who tops the list of nice people in the world.

He's warm and friendly in an old-world Fiorentino style, and if you happen to find him in Badiani (he's not there all the time because he's retired), say hello and show him this book.

Pomposi's journey to master gelato maker was an indirect one. In 1940, he finished his compulsory education and took a job collecting milk from the local farmers of his hometown Quarrata and delivering it to a clearing center on the road to Florence. In the evenings he continued his schooling.

During this time, one of his relatives in Quarrata started a club for working men and farmers that served homemade gelato—young Pomposi helped make it. This was the beginning of his interest in gelato.

Later on, after a variety of jobs, he was working for a fabric manufacturer near Prato—weaving fabric on a home loom and delivering it to the factory in his small van—when he thought about buying a bar in the *centro storico* of Florence. "On

August 15, 1958, I came to Florence and went to look at Bar Fiorenza on Via Calzaiuoli and talked with the owner. An hour later I bought it, and the adventure began," says Pomposi.

At first he didn't make gelato in Bar Fiorenza, although it had been in the back of his mind since working in the club in Quarrata. Then, in 1961, Pomposi bought a gelato machine at a Milan trade show and experimented with selling gelato in the summer. "Eventually we made it in the winter, too," says Pomposi. "There wasn't much request in the beginning. We kept at it, and little by little we sold gelato all year round."

Bar Fiorenza became Bar Fiorenza-Gelateria Pomposi. And word spread. As his business grew, *gelato artigianale* itself began to disappear, replaced by *gelato industriale* made in large batches with artificial ingredients by big companies. In fact, says Pomposi, there weren't many gelaterias left in Florence when he started.

He was not the only one concerned with this development. In 1960, *Il Comitato nazionale per la difesa e la diffusione del gelato artigianale* (or committee for the defense and diffusion of handmade gelato) was formed to single-handedly save this genuine and fresh product. Pomposi joined the group, along with other colleagues (some included in this book) and became very active in organizing provincial and national versions of the committee.

"I started making gelato out of passion," says Pomposi—which is clearly an understatement if you spend any time with him. The old joke applies here: Next to the word "passionate" in the dictionary is Pomposi's face.

"With our organization, he says, "we raised the status of the gelato maker to a professional. We improved his image with competitions, certifications, and round tables. As awareness of *gelato artigianale* increased, we gained ground. True gelato lovers began to notice the difference between the homemade and the mass-produced."

Like all businesses in the *centro storico*, Bar Fiorenza suffered a setback during the great flood of November 1966. The basement was flooded with mud and oily residue, which covered the equipment, machinery, and twelve tubs of gelato that had just been prepared (changing their flavor considerably). Clean-up took 20 days, using shovels, rags, and disinfectant, and, as Pomposi puts it, "a bottle of whiskey at hand to keep everyone disinfected—on the inside."

Over the years Bar Fiorenza-Gelateria Pomposi prospered, and, in 1993, Orazio Pomposi bought another business, Pasticceria Gelateria Badiani. It had been owned by a corporation and run by a manager for about 20 years, and consequently had slipped a long way from where it was when Idilio Badiani started the place in 1933. Pomposi brought the quality of products back to their former high level. In 1996, he and his family decided two gelaterias were one too many, so they sold the business on Via Calzaiuoli.

Badiani sits on Via dei Mille in an area developed between the wars (1920–1935), a short way from the *centro storico* and not far from the Campo di Marte sports stadium. It's a pleasant, upper-middle-class neighborhood without many tourists. Badiani's tasteful interior features a small, elegantly curved bar and impeccable display cases filled with tempting pastries and gelato.

Paolo Pomposi took over as gelato maker from his father in 1996. When Paolo is not in the *laboratorio*, he likes to ski with his wife and three sons: 5, 15, and 17.

Making gelato must agree with him, because he looks 10 years younger than his forty-five years. He is the one with the dry sense of humor, always in the *laboratorio* creating exquisite gelato both from family recipes and those passed down in Idilio Badiani's secret book—flavors such as *crema, cioccolato, cioccoriso, cremarancio, fedora, Malaga,* and *Buontalenti*.

The Pomposi family is especially proud of their delicate and utterly enchanting Buontalenti flavor, which tastes of eggs and cream and flowers. The flavor is named after Bernardo Buontalenti (1531–1608), a Florentine of many talents: civil and military architect, hydraulic engineer, city planner, set designer, and inventor of artificial fire and the merry-go-round. He also designed Villa di Pratolino, Fortezza del Belvedere, and the corridor leading from the Pitti Palace to the Uffizi. In his spare time, he applied his obsessive personality to making crystal and ceramic vases, glass, and jewelry—and to cooking.

The Medici loved this guy. He not only designed their buildings and helped plan their city, but he could also organize a great party, which they asked him to do when the Spanish Embassy opened in Florence. They wanted an event that would impress "these foreign blockheads who were—to make things even worse—Spanish."

Buontalenti outdid himself, filling the streets and piazzas with thousands of torches, and presenting a splendid banquet that included a large credenza of cold sweets. At the time, frozen desserts had progressed only as far as a sorbet (water, sugar, and fruit). Buontalenti pushed the envelope by using a milk base with egg yolks, along with honey and a splash of wine, to create gelato as we know it today. Adding milk and eggs gave the frozen sweet a smooth, full flavor.

The famous architect would be proud of his namesake at Badiani, which won first prize in 1970 at the first competition between all the gelato makers in Florence for the best version of Buontalenti gelato.

Rivaling the Buontalenti story, another gelato legend has it that Ruggeri, a Florentine cook and chicken seller, originated modern gelato.

Ruggeri accidentally broke into the fame game when he entered a cooking contest at the Medici court. The theme was "most unusual dish." He prepared a frozen mixture of cream, fruit, and *zabaglione* (egg yolks, sugar, and Marsala wine)—and won. The judges exclaimed, "We have never tasted such a delicious sweet."

Ruggeri became the "flavor of the month." He put on wonderful displays at the royal banquets and began giving new shape to his creations with a sort of gelato sculpting. Catherine de' Medici took Ruggeri with her when she moved to Paris to marry Enrico d'Orleans, and there the maestro created a masterful dessert for her nuptials on October 20, 1553. Fame, though, was a mixed blessing for Ruggeri. He was both envied and hated by many Parisian cooks, and even, he claimed, robbed and assaulted because of his reputation. Soon it became too much for him; he wrote a note to Catherine: "With your permission, I'd like to return to my chickens. I'll be left in peace and people will be happy enjoying my gelato."

Badiani is also known for its *semifreddo*, which as Paolo Pomposi explains, is different from gelato. "*Semifreddo* has a cream base. You don't add milk or water. With gelato you use milk, which is 93 percent water. It gets colder than the cream-based *semifreddo* and feels colder in your mouth. The name *semifreddo* means less *freddo* (cold), or semicold. For this reason, people tend to eat it more in the winter. The flavor's more intense."

"In the past 30 years, you see *semifreddo* sold alongside of gelato. Before, that wasn't the case. Not everyone makes semifreddo. To make it well takes a lot of time… much longer than gelato."

At Badiani, pastry is also a big draw—partly due to Pino, the highly talented and temperamental pastry chef. He didn't want his picture taken for this book because he was covered with flour and his work area was dirty. In fact, the *pasticceria*, or bakery, (along with the gelato kitchen) is so clean you could literally eat off of any surface, including the floor. Good pastry chefs are in demand around Florence, and Pino could get a job anywhere. But he has stayed with Badiani for ten years because he's very content.

Ask for the pastry called *brutti ma buoni* (ugly but good)—a delicious little squiggle made with almond paste.

You can't have pastry, or gelato for that matter, without a good espresso (caffé as the Italians call it). Badiani uses a local roast that reflects the perfectionist approach to everything they sell. This is excellent coffee.

According to Pomposi, the best coffee comes from an espresso machine where the *barista* (operator) uses a hand lever to draw the water through the coffee. In Naples, the bars still use many of these machines. "I discovered something I didn't know about coffee a few months ago when I made a trip there," says Pomposi.

"At Badiani, we don't automatically add sugar, but in Naples they always put a teaspoon of sugar in the cup before they draw the coffee. I asked a barista, 'Why do you do this?' He told me the first drop that comes from the machine has more aroma than all the others. If the cup is empty, the drop falls into the cup and dissipates. Sugar concentrates and captures that first drop and the major part of the aroma."

Visit this pleasant spot and rub elbows with the locals, a famous soccer player or two from the nearby stadium, and maybe a tourist like yourself.

You need a break from the crowds in the centro storico. *Go to the train station. Ask the transit guys in the little house in front which bus goes to Via dei Mille. Take it. Get off at your stop. Go directly to Badiani and enjoy their rich pistacchio gelato… or caffé-flavored* semifreddo, *rich yet so light that it almost floats into the mouth… or a* pinguino, *an ice cream bar that looks like a penguin. Afterwards, a tiny cup of the best espresso you'll find anywhere. Badiani also makes an ideal stop on the way back from Fiesole.*

Cavini

Piazza delle Cure, 19-23/r
055 587489
Open 7AM—1AM, Tuesday to Sunday
Closed Mondays

Giuseppe Cavini came to Florence from Rome in 1926 and started a gelateria on what was, at the time, the outskirts of the city: the corner of Via Boccaccio and Via Borghini. It's not clear why he left Rome. Maybe he wanted a change, or perhaps it was simply opportunity—there were few gelaterias in Florence. Anyway, within a short time his excellent gelato became well known.

Eleven years later, Cavini moved his gelato to larger premises in a new building on nearby Piazza delle Cure. The elegant old Villa Cintolesi was torn down and its gardens removed to make room for Cavini's new home.

Gelateria Cavini grew steadily; it was considered among the best in Florence. Everything came to a sudden halt in 1940 when World War II exploded across Italy. Rationing made it very difficult to find basic ingredients for gelato, so Giuseppe Cavini adapted and sold polenta instead.

In 1943, tragedy struck close to home: the Cavini's youngest son was killed during an ill-conceived Allied bombing raid on the nearby Campo di Marte train station. The family never recovered.

The war ended, and the Cavini family rebuilt the business, but it never attained its prewar level of success. Increased competition—from new gelaterias and from gelato made with artificial ingredients and a ready-made base instead of fresh milk and eggs—took its toll. Giuseppe Cavini kept at it, though, until he died in 1962. His wife died in 1965 and the business went to their sons.

Enter the Fedi family in 1969: Giorgio and his wife Mis bought the neglected gelateria and put themselves to work. For that matter, the whole family pitched in. Old-time customers remember the two daughters Susanna and Liliana, aged 10 and 12, helping behind the counter so their parents could get a short rest.

These were difficult years of hard work and *sacrifici* (sacrifices), but also satisfying because the Fiorentini rediscovered Cavini and its marvelous gelato. (Italians often talk about *sacrifici*, especially when it comes to having children. More than one? *Ma che sacrificio!*).

Shortly after buying the gelateria, Fedi received the equivalent of an Oscar for the best *gelato al caffè* at the Fiera Internazionale di Padova. "I kept Cavini's way of making gelato… using only the best materials. The fruit is real fruit. The milk is fresh. Everything is genuine," says Fedi. In 1975, Giorgio Fedi took over the complete gelato making—up until that point, the Cavini sons were still involved in

production. Fedi hired new workers such as the *gelataio* (gelato maker) Mario, who is still with him.

The two daughters grew up, apprenticed at the cash register, and learned to make gelato in the *laboratorio*. Business continued to improve, but by 1987, after 50 years in the same building, the gelateria showed its age. "I rebuilt the *laboratorio* and the shop interior was completely renovated," says Fedi. The result is a bright, cheery, and efficient establishment.

The next milestone came four years later when Susanna's husband, Michele, and Liliana's husband, Claudio, became active in the gelateria. Fedi explains, "I got them involved in the business because it needed some new blood, younger blood. And they've been improving things very nicely." On June 1, 1992, Giorgio Fedi and the

two couples formed a *società* (corporation), and with the business in good hands, Fedi and his wife retired.

Giorgio Fedi is a chatty, bright-eyed man in his seventies who will gladly talk about his years in the gelateria, but if you want to see him light up, ask about his music collection. In the comfortable apartment he shares with his wife, there are huge, built-in shelves filled with more than 5,000 records. He loves jazz, especially musicians such as composer, arranger, and trombonist Slide Hampton and saxophonists Lou Donaldson and James Moody, both of whom he met during a visit to New York City.

Fedi is especially proud of his rare V-Discs—records created by the United States government music company, V-Disc Records, specifically for the American military. This oddball label came about as the result of the musicians strike during World War II. The American Federation of Musicians wanted residuals for records played on the radio or in a jukebox. The four major recording companies—Decca, RCA, Columbia, and Capital—more or less said, "Tough." So the musicians struck on July 31, 1942. The big four could make no new records, which meant soldiers missed out on new songs and singers.

As a result, Lt. George Vincent, an enterprising officer assigned to the Armed Services Radio Service, got permission to form a company that would provide current recorded music to soldiers and sailors. For a few years, the US government was the sole producer of new releases of popular music.

The musicians' union agreed to a special strike waiver, as long as Vincent guaranteed that the V-Discs were not sold anywhere or used for commercial purposes—and were destroyed after the war.

There were, however, other problems to overcome. The old 78s of the day were made with shellac, and the Japanese had taken over French Indochina, the source of this imported substance.

And even if available in unlimited supply, shellac made extremely fragile records; the ones shipped to service men overseas usually arrived in many pieces.

Vincent found the substitute: a more durable mixture of Vinylite (used in insulation and life rafts) and Formvar, a polyvinyl. He also expanded the size of the records from a standard 10 inches to 12 for six full minutes of music. V-Discs were

an immediate hit—delivering big band tunes, jazz, classical, semi-classical, and swing performed by stars such as Glenn Miller, Benny Goodman, Bing Crosby, Frank Sinatra, Woody Herman, Count Basie, and Louis Armstrong. All free of charge to music-starved GIs.

The strike ended after a couple of years, when the music companies finally gave in to the union demands. But V-discs continued until 1949.

Most V-Discs were destroyed per the agreement with the musicians' union. It's reported that the FBI (on a slow day in the crime business) confiscated the V-Discs that servicemen tried to smuggle home. An employee at an LA record company even went to jail for illegal possession of more than 2,000 V-Discs. Nevertheless, some of the records survived the V-Disc Inquisition, and the Library of Congress has a complete set.

The interesting thing about the V-Discs is that they paired up musicians who were ordinarily unable to play together because of limiting record contracts: Judy Garland sang "Somewhere Over the Rainbow" accompanied by Tommy Dorsey. Ella Fitzgerald and Buddy Rich scatted their way through "Blue Skies." Abbott and Costello did their "Who's on First" routine on the same V-Disc as a baseball medley played by the Brooklyn Dodgers' organist.

Your V-Disc history lesson complete, you may ask yourself: Who will I find at

Cavini? Lots of locals, a few tourists, and the occasional Italian celebrity. Roberto Zaccaria, president of RAI, the Italian state broadcasting company, has been known to show up (have your audition ready). You also might see Leonardo Pieraccioni, who wrote and acted in *Il Mio West*, an attempt to revive the spaghetti western. The film starred the strange twosome of Harvey Keitel and David Bowie. Carlo Monni, dubbed the Italian Brando, comes by; he often works with Roberto Benigni. Then, for the John Steinbeck fans there is Piero Pelu, an Italian rocker who has read Steinbeck's *Tortilla Flat* 10 times during 10 different periods of his life because it is an exultation of friendship. And occasionally, a player for Fiorentina, the Florence soccer team, drops by for a cup or a cone.

Here's another chance to escape the crowds in the *centro storico*. You could walk, but the #1 or #7 bus is better. Cavini sits on Piazza delle Cure at the end of Via dei Mille.

The gelateria creates its own music with a symphony of gelato flavors—50 in all. Where to begin? The strawberry is exquisite, as is the orange and cream, but for the capolavoro (masterpiece) it's a toss-up between hazelnut and walnut. Both rich and grainy. If you favor pistachio, there are two kinds; Italian and Sicilian. For something really different, try the riso *(rice). The best thing to do is ask for small sampler cups of all the flavors. Be careful when you get in line—one time, not that long ago, the painter Zimarelli, a bizarre character, came in to buy gelato on horseback.*

· 4 ·

FILAROCCA &
PIAZZA BECCARIA

Hop a bus or take a long walk—these residential areas are worth a visit. See how the Fiorentini *live in Filarocca or check out the quiet neighborhoods around Piazza Beccaria. You'll be surprised how quickly the tourists vanish. Other than you, they don't get out this way.*

Ciolli

Via Ramazzini, 35-37
055 677554
Open 9:30ᴀᴍ—midnight,
May to September
Open 9:30ᴀᴍ—9ᴘᴍ, October to April
Closed Tuesdays

*V*isiting Ciolli is like time travel. Step into the gelateria and you enter an ice cream parlor from 1954— the year the building was constructed by Mario Ciolli, a contractor and son of the original owner. The senior Ciolli first opened a latteria at the same spot, in a house with the shop underneath and a garden in back. The year was 1930 and he delivered his milk and butter with a horse-drawn cart.

Eventually, he began to make gelato, which soon became his best seller. For that reason, the new shop featured the latest, 1954 gelato-refrigeration technology: a large tank filled with brine and a natural gas motor that chills the brine and circulates it through metal tubes winding around the inside of the stainless steel wells holding the tubs of gelato. The coolant must be brine made with a special salt that keeps the water from freezing. This original system is still in use today. So now, when you see Carlo Piattoli open one of the stainless steel lids on the charming old counter, and dig into a container of his marvelous gelato, you know why it stays cold.

Carlo was born and raised in the neighborhood and worked as a *barista* before he bought the gelateria in 1966 from the Ciolli family, who had no heir apparent. As Carlo says, "It's much more satisfying to make gelato than be a *barista*. To make gelato at an *alto livello* (high level) is like being an artist. "

Carlo's son Fabio agrees; he runs the business with his father. Not only is there a strong resemblance between the two (obviously from the same tub of gelato), but they finish each other's sentences. "It is especially satisfying," continues Fabio, "when you serve someone and they come back with two or three friends. This is a compliment that repays us more than money. Also, many people return after 10 or 20 years and they say, 'This is the exact same gelato I ate as a child.'"

"It's always the same," adds Carlo. "We have the same style gelato that was made 50 years ago. The process is still the same. This is very, very important."

Filarocca (also known as Coverciano), the area around Ciolli, was built up right after World War II. Before that it was comprised of a few houses and villas on the periphery of Florence, but more or less in *campagna* (in the country) at the "end of the bus line."

Nearby you'll find Campo di Marte, a large sports complex developed in 1932. Prior to this date it would have been tough to play baseball or soccer on its fields because a biplane would have very likely landed in the middle of the game. The reason: In 1910, the Italian military authority decided to use the area (a large meadow) for "*Esperimenti di Navigazione Aerea*" (experiments in aerial navigation). From then through most of the 1920s it was the first airport of Florence, which soon became outdated as airplane technology developed. By 1928, plans were afoot to move the airport to a more suitable location, and in 1930, the present Aeroporto di Peretola opened.

Nearby on the Via Gabriele D'Annunzio sits the Centro Tecnico di Coverciano, a huge national sports clinic for Italy's favorite pastime—soccer. It includes five playing fields, two gyms, two tennis courts, a pool, and a coaching lab. The Italian national soccer teams train here.

Ciolli's residential neighborhood is off the tourist track, yet not far from the *centro storico*. "The tourists are sometimes afraid to leave the center of Florence, especially if they don't speak Italian," says Fabio. "Few tourists come here. Usually they hear about us through word of mouth. Sometimes language students come to Florence and rent apartments in this zone—Americans, Australians, and Japanese."

When not dishing out gelato, Fabio Piattoli rides motorcycles and watches movies—of course, not at the same time. He describes himself as an aficionado of American cinema, especially of the 1940s and 1950s. "My favorites from that period are *Casablanca* and *The Maltese Falcon*... both are in my DVD collection. My wife also likes movies, although she won't watch two or three films on a Friday night like I do.

I like all genres: science fiction, action adventure, comedy. A glass of wine, a pizza, and a good movie... *l'ottima serata* (the best evening)."

Fabio bombs around on a Honda XL 600, and he's taken many summer holidays touring France, Italy, and Germany by motorcycle. "You see the world in a more intimate way compared to the car," he says.

Fabio and his wife both have a dream that does not include gelato. It started a couple of years ago when they got a white female boxer called Naomi. Fabio says, "We both love dogs and my wife likes animals in general. I'd love to have a dog school. My wife is a physical therapist and she's been thinking about studying physical therapy for dogs. There are vets and others who actually do this. First she'd have to get some experience and then we'd offer it at our school. It's not easy because we both work... but maybe some day."

There's life outside the centro storico. *Take bus #6 from the train station and discover for yourself—it stops almost in front of Ciolli. Go inside this fine example of 1950s architecture. Admire the simple stainless steel counter, and then order gelato from Carlo or Fabio Piattoli. Not many tourists stumble on the place, so you'll feel special. Try the* bacio *(tastes like the famous* baci *from Perugina) or the* nocciola *or Ciolli's original flavor—*panna gelato. Panna *means cream in Italian; this one is not for lightweight gelato lovers. By the way, the big Honda motorcycle parked in front belongs to Fabio. When you finish your gelato, talk motorcycles with him. Afterwards, visit Motorama, the big motorcycle accessory store on Via Mannelli, 79. Nobody designs motorcycle gear like the Italians.*

Gelateria Veneta

Piazza Beccaria, 7/r
055 2343370
Open 8AM—8PM in winter
8AM—midnight in summer
Open daily

The present location of Piazza Beccaria was a place to avoid in the year 1300. Condemned prisoners from Florence's notorious Stinche Prison were transported to this empty field to be hung, burned, or beheaded.

In the middle of the piazza sits Porta alla Croce, one of the old city gates. Not much is known about its history—Michele di Ridolfo painted the fresco of the Madonna and child on the inside, and on the outside there is a small wooden door with the mysterious sign: *Capo dell' Emissario* (head emissary).

Ironically, in the late 1860s, when Giuseppe Poggi laid out the piazza and surrounding area as part of his grand urban renewal plan for the city, it was named after Cesare Beccaria (1738–1794). At the age of 26, this forward-thinking criminologist, economist, and jurist from Milan wrote the famous *Essay on Crimes and Punishment*, one of the first arguments against capital punishment and inhuman treatment of criminals.

About the time Piazza Beccaria was given its name, people from the Veneto began migrating across Italy and the world to make their living as *gelatai* (gelato makers). This continued into the 1920s when Giovanni Arnoldo, the grandfather of owners Daniele and Stefano Arnoldo, came to Florence and opened Gelateria Veneta. The first location was on Via Milazzo in 1924. He then moved to Via Gioberti, and finally, in 1929, he settled into the current location, a late-1800s building on Piazza Beccaria. Giovanni's brother Virgilio started Gelateria Alpina (also in this book) in 1929.

Veneta's *laboratorio* (kitchen) and its gelato-making equipment have come a long way since those early days when *salamoia* (brine made from ice water and a special salt) circulated through metal tubing to keep the gelato cold. Today, along with the latest refrigeration technology, you'll find a *pastorizzatore* (pasteurizer), an amazing machine that heats 3–6 liters of the liquid to 85 degrees centigrade and cools it down to 4 degrees in less than two hours. "First we prepare a liquid base of milk, eggs, and sugar, then we pasteurize it," says Daniele Arnoldo. "When you work with eggs and milk you must do that. Once at 4 degrees, it will keep for a few days.

"When the base is ready, we add the *nocciola* or *pistacchio* paste or whatever flavor we are going to use, and put these ingredients in a *mantecatore* (a giant freestanding mixer). Within ten to fifteen minutes, we have gelato that is ready to sell."

The Arnoldo brothers stick to classic flavors, even though sometimes customers ask for strange things like vegetable gelato. "We've experimented with asparagus, potato, carrot, and parsley," says Daniele. "But you have to add lots of water and this dilutes the taste. In the last year, *gelato di soya* (soy ice cream) became fashionable—low calorie, no milk or sugar. I tried making it, but again, the flavor just isn't there."

Using their grandfather's recipes, Daniele and his brother Stefano begin creating fresh batches of gelato and *torta di gelato* (ice cream cake) at 7AM. It's difficult for two families to make a living from one gelateria—especially since many gelaterias open every year, using a prepackaged base and flavorings. However, according to Daniele, those businesses don't make good gelato, so many of them end up closing in a short time.

Outside of work, Daniele spends time with his family, and he raises dogs—an Irish setter named Tommy and two basset hounds: Whiskey and Birba. Older brother Stefano likes to hunt wild boar during the winter.

Veneta's client base has always been the regulars who pass on the gelateria from one generation to the next. Among this group of loyal *gelato artigianale* lovers was writer Aldo Palazzeschi (1885–1974)—he lived in an apartment directly above Alpina. Palazzeschi, relatively unknown outside of Italy, wrote extremely imaginative poetry, novels, short stories, and memoirs. Another regular, writer and poet Eugenio Montale (1896–1981), lived at Viale Amendola, 38 on the other side of the piazza; he received the 1975 Nobel Prize in Literature for his distinctive

poetry. And last but not least, Totò (1898–1967), the beloved Neapolitan comic famous for his broad humor, animated face, and many Italian "B" comedies, dropped by often in the 1930s.

As for tourists, Daniele says, "They comprise maybe ten percent of the business. They don't come because the tourist maps don't show anything here. They go as far as Santa Croce and then turn around."

According to owner Daniele Arnoldo, ninety percent of the people in the Veneto know how to make excellent gelato. Gelateria Veneta's name reflects this tradition of fine gelato. You'll want to come here for classic flavors like crema, cioccolato, pistacchio, *and* nocciola. *Take electric bus "A" from the train station to Veneta's front door—about a 15-minute ride.*

· 5 ·

OUTSIDE THE CITY

*O*r, as the Italians say, *fuori città*. You may want to get out of town for a day—here's where to go: Visit the charming hill-town of Fiesole, which has looked down on Florence (in more ways than one) ever since the Romans conquered it 2,000 years ago. A little further away and to the east, at the confluence of the Arno and Sieve Rivers, you'll find the pleasant town of Pontassieve.

Bar Sottani

Via Forlivese, 93
S. Francesco di Pelago (FI)
055 8314446
Open 6:30AM—midnight,
Thursday to Tuesday
Closed Wednesdays

*L*uckily for gelato lovers, Giancarlo Sottani is never satisfied. This was apparent back in July of 1965, when his family bought a bar at San Francisco di Pelago near Pontassieve. "I was 17 years old at the time. I felt like an intermediary supplying products and drinks… clients came in, drank a coffee or beer, and left. There was nothing of me here," says Sottani, a pleasant middle-aged man who looks like a *gelataio* (gelato maker), even without his white uniform.

"I didn't get any satisfaction in the bar until we made gelato," he continues. " I have to create. You have to do something that turns you on, or you get old.

"We got to a place where we had to decide—do we make pizza or gelato? With my family, I built a small *laboratorio*, and we bought the tools to make gelato."

How did he actually learn to make *gelato artigianale*? "Lots of trial and error," he says. But after the first year it was clear that the family made the right choice. Their gelato was a great success; they went from eight flavors, to ten, to the twenty they have today.

"We keep trying to innovate, to create new flavors," says Sottani. "We test them out with the customers. If they don't like them, we discontinue them. Always using

high-quality ingredients from the area—milk, eggs, all kinds of fresh fruit... even vegetables. The other day we tried wild asparagus gelato. For 40 years we've been doing it this way. Always experimenting."

Bar Sottani sits on the outskirts of Pontassieve, a small city about 12 kilometers east of Florence, at the convergence of the Arno and Sieve rivers. The city's history begins in the late Middle Ages when the Da Quona family from Florence laid claim to the area for political and economic reasons. In the early 1200s, the family gave some of its property to the archdiocese of Florence, which built a church dedicated to Sant'Angelo (the holy angel); later, around 1375, the Republic of Florence built a castle on this strategic location, calling it Castel Sant'Angelo. Only three gates remain from the castle: Porta Fiorentina, Porta Felicaia, and Porta dell'Orologio.

The little town that grew up around the castle was called Borgo di Castel Sant'Angelo, which eventually changed to Ponte a Sieve or Pontassieve (bridge at the

Sieve) because of the bridge over the Sieve river. For centuries, the bridge was an important link on the road between Florence and Arezzo. Floods damaged it many times; the worst was in 1548 and again in November of 1844 (only four years after a complete reconstruction). Finally, a new, more solid structure of three arches to withstand the raging waters was finished in 1888—and stood until World War II when the Allies bombed it, along with Pontassieve's important railroad hub. The bridge you see today was rebuilt in 1948, partly from the remains of the old bridge.

Over the centuries, Pontassieve has been an agricultural center for wine, oil, corn, beans, and mulberries; a center for production of hemp and linen; and by the early 1900s an important railroad hub.

Today, there is still a mixture of commerce, but you're probably most interested in the wine and olive oil from the surrounding region and the artisans who create leather shoes, jackets, and purses. You get a better deal on leather goods out here than in Florence.

Bar Sottani is near a leather factory and across the street from a hospital. The original owners built the bar in 1957 to serve the hospital;

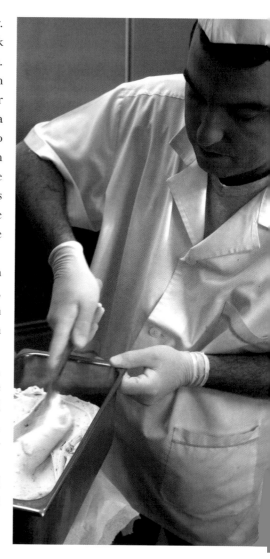

there was a bar, restaurant, grocery store, and a small hotel upstairs where the Sottani family now lives.

During the warm weather, Sottani puts on entertainment. "We have music and singing in the gardens but we have to be careful because of the hospital. They don't want a lot of noise. Three or four times in the summer we have concerts that finish at midnight. And with

these evenings, we usually have promotional events like spumanti tasting, or we create a theme—recently we did a Cuban evening," says Sottani.

Pontassieve had its moment of glory in the 1950s when local restaurant Girarrosto was discovered and put the little town on the map. Gino Maglioni opened the rustic eatery in 1952, in an area of the world known for great food. Soon Girarrosto had a reputation as the best of the best, offering roast game and simple recipes in the style of the original *cucina povera* (poor man's cuisine) of the region. Part of the appeal was the show: huge pieces of meat turned on a huge spit in the main hall, and, according to Giancarlo Sottani, "Dead wild boar lined up on the sidewalk in front of the restaurant waited to be roasted... the specialty of the house." Doctors, truck drivers, young couples, families, businessmen, and tourists—everyone came to eat and drink. During "La Dolce Vita," the restaurant was on the circuit and celebrity diners included Ava Gardner, Vittorio De Sica, Sophia Loren, and Marcello Mastroianni.

Giorgio La Pira, the colorful mayor of Florence from 1951–1958 and 1961–1965, was also a regular. During World War II as a member of the *partigiani*, La Pira printed an antifascist underground newsletter. This did not make him popular with the Germans, but they were never able to arrest him. Later, as a peace activist during the cold war, he promoted worldwide disarmament.

In the 1990s, the original owners sold the restaurant; a renovated and updated version exists today, still serving excellent food.

Sottani worries about what will happen when he retires. The plan is to hand off the business to his son, Gianluca, who works with him now. "My son went to a *scuola alberghiera* (hotel school). Since he's been a little boy he's been around the business, and I've taught him what I know. He's interested, but I don't shove it down his throat."

The problem according to Sottani: It's difficult to find someone who wants to carry on a tradition of eighteen-hour days and delicate precise work in the culinary equivalent of a clean room. "You have to treat *gelato artigianale* like you treat a baby. It needs all your attention, all your passion. You have to be dedicated. If your hand or sponge is the slightest bit dirty or contaminated, you have problems."

And the work never ends. When the doors close, it's time to clean under the wooden platforms in the *laboratorio*, plan for the next day, and count the money. Sottani goes to bed about 12:30AM. and wakes up at 6AM.

At the end of September, he takes some time off, however, as he puts it, "When I'm not working, I think about what I should be doing." He's typical of the old breed of gelato maker devoted to creating the best homemade product. He prowls trade shows and visits other gelato makers, always searching for new ideas. His work is gelato. His hobby is gelato. His life is gelato.

How about a day trip to eat some wonderful gelato? (It's as good an excuse as any.) Pontassieve is only twelve kilometers from Firenze. Check out the old part of Pontassieve, then go to Bar Sottani, only one kilometer out of town. Try the yogurt with fruit (lots of other toppings, too) and the fruit-flavored gelato, made with only fruit, water, and sugar. No milk or cream, but you'd never know it. How do they do it? Espresso and cappuccino are also good. Locals love this place.

Pasticceria Marino

Piazza San Domenico, 7/8
Fiesole (FI)
055 599716
Open everyday, 8AM to 6PM

*F*irst, the Romans conquered Fiesole. The great Julius Caesar pitched camp along the Arno and eventually, after much time and difficulty, managed to defeat the Etruscan hill town. His Roman camp, named Florentia, eventually grew into the city of Florence.

Roughly 1,000 years later, in 1010, the Fiorentini decided to give it a try. According to *Cronache Fiorentine*, written in 1300 by the 20-year-old historian Giovanni Villani, Florence wanted to vanquish its stubborn, independent archrival Fiesole, which had the military and psychological advantage of the hilltop location. The strategy was for the Fiorentini to become the new best friends of the people of Fiesole. This accomplished, later on during a festival in Fiesole, the Florentine army snuck into the city and took control. The inhabitants were allowed to leave before most of Fiesole—except for a small fortress, a bishop's palace, and some churches—was destroyed. (The religious Fiorentini were probably hedging their bets).

Today the Fiorentini are interested in Fiesole for its stunning view of Florence and the fact that for most of the year it's an escape from the maddening tourist crowds. Only 8 kilometers from the center of Florence, the hill-town is definitely worth a visit.

As you climb the winding Via Vecchia Fiesolana, remember to stop halfway up the hill at the hamlet of San Domenico and Piazza San Domenico. The reasons are twofold: gastronomical and historical.

We'll begin with the gastronomical—pastry and gelato at Pasticceria Marino, located on the right side on Piazza San Domenico (not really a piazza, but more of a small plateau on the hill).

The owner is Sebastiano Marino, an upbeat, intelligent man, who bought the business in June of 2002 from Antonio Villani, a third-generation *gelataio*. Like many family-business owners in Italy, Villani carefully interviewed prospective buyers to find someone he thought would maintain the quality of his products—an audition of sorts. In this case, Sebastiano Marino got the part.

"When I bought this place," says Marino, "I had to learn to make gelato. It's not a lot different than making pastry, which I've done for almost 30 years. With gelato, you're basically making a frozen sweet… and every *gelataio* has his method. The former owner was a *grande maestro* (grand master). He'd been making gelato for many, many years and learned from his father. I worked with him for three months and learned his secrets."

When Sebastiano Marino entered the pastry trade, there were no schools. From 1974–1982, he apprenticed with the best master pastry makers he could find, and

then on January 1, 1982, he opened his own business in the *centro storico*. Eight years later, he sold it and bought a second place, which he had for twelve years until he purchased Pasticceria Marino.

Sicilian by birth, Marino grew up in Florence—his mother was a nurse and his father, a *polizzioto* (policeman). "When I was little and my father had to take care of me, he would take me to the *questura* (police station), give me an old typewriter, and I'd peck away on it," says Marino. "It was not like today with computers and all the technology. In those days, they had only one radio. Things were a little more primitive and a lot more relaxed."

Also in those days, there was only one police corps, and each policeman had four completely different uniforms. "He worked night and day. They'd telephone him and say, 'Today you are Vigili Urbani. Tomorrow, Squadra Mobile.'"

How many types of police forces do the Italians have? Quite a few—probably a

dozen, depending on who you ask. Here are some of them: Carabinieri, Polizia di Stato, Polizia Municipale, Polizia Provinciale, Polizia Penitenziaria, Guardia di Finanza, Guardia Ecologica, and Corpo Forestale. As you can imagine, many of their duties overlap.

The two most important are the *polizia*, who wear blue uniforms, and the *carabinieri*, who wear very cool black uniforms with a red stripe running down the outside of the trouser legs. The latter, a military and police corps started by Vittorio Emanuele I on July 13, 1814, is also the most elite. Originally, the *carabinieri* were equipped with carbines—hence the name. They have many specialized units, including a high-tech, art-theft group called *Nucleo Tutela Patrimonio Artistico*.

Sebastiano Marino spends long hours in his business. After work, when he has time, he rides his horse Giada (Jade). "She's old now. I got her when she was 5 and I've had her for 22 years. I keep her nearby on a friend's property. Ten years ago I rode more. I'd go home after work, eat, rest, and then go for a ride—almost every day. Six or seven years ago I got into flying kites. For me, horseback riding and kites are similar: I go someplace quiet, out in nature, and they clear my mind."

Once you've enjoyed the gastronomical side of San Domenico, explore its history. Close to the pasticceria are Fiesole's first cathedral, Badia Fiesolana, and the Convento di San Domenico (Convent of Saint Dominic), founded in 1406 and inhabited by both monks and nuns at different periods. The most illustrious San Domenico alumnus is painter Fra Angelico (1400–1455), who entered the religious community in 1420, and after learning to illustrate manuscripts, produced his first paintings in the form of altarpieces and frescoes. Fra Angelico spent much time at San Domenico, eventually becoming the prior.

Throughout the centuries, Via Vecchia Fiesolana has always been the only road to Fiesole. "In the old days before cars, it took a long time to get up here," says Marino. "You stopped, rested at San Domenico, and then went on to Fiesole. It was like another world in the 1930s and even after the war. People went down to Florence on foot with a cart, did their business, and returned in a day.

"It's still nice in this area. It never really changes because they can't build up here. It's hidden and very expensive—lots of villas and exclusive homes with walls that are 3 meters high and completely closed gates. In Emilia, for example, you can see through all the gates. That's the difference between Toscana and the rest of Italy. In Toscana, they're very concerned with privacy—everything is *bello* (beautiful) and *nascosto* (hidden)."

The clientele at Pasticceria Marino includes tourists, locals, and students from the Scuola di Musica di Fiesole. You also may find teachers and research staff from the nearby European University Institute, set up by the EC in 1972 to promote high-level research in history, law, economics, and political and social science.

Specialty of the house? According to the owner, "Everything is special. If I don't like it, I don't sell it." The coffee and pastry are wonderful. In the summer, try the fruit gelato—sugar, water, fresh fruit, and a little farina di carruba *(carob powder) to hold everything together. Take bus #7 from the train station (a 20-minute ride). Sebastiano Marino will be glad to see you.*

CAFÉ LISTINGS

Badiani
Viale dei Mille, 20/r
055 578682
Open 7AM—1AM
7AM—midnight, Sunday
Closed Tuesdays

Bar Sottani
Via Forlivese, 93
S. Francesco di Pelago (FI)
055 8314446
Open 6:30AM—midnight,
Thursday to Tuesday
Closed Wednesdays

I Barberi
Via Palestro at Via Il Prato
055 212604
Open 7AM—7PM, Monday to Saturday
Closed Sundays

Bottega del Gelato
Via Por Santa Maria, 33/r
055 3296550
Open 7AM—9PM in winter

7AM—1AM in summer
Open daily

Caffè Concerto Paszkowski
Piazza della Repubblica, 6/r
055 210236
Open 7AM—1:30 AM, Tuesday to Sunday
Closed Mondays

Caffè Gilli
Piazza della Repubblica, 39/r
055 213896
Open 8AM—midnight, Wednesday
to Monday
Closed Tuesdays

Caffè Pasticceria Rivoire
Via Vacchereccia, 4
(Piazza della Signoria)
055 214412
Open 8AM—midnight, Tuesday
to Sunday
Closed Mondays

Cavini

Piazza delle Cure, 19-23/r
055 587489
Open 7AM—1AM
Closed Mondays

Ciolli

Via Ramazzini, 35-37
055 677554
Open 9:30AM—midnight,
May to September
Open 9:30AM—9PM, October to April
Closed Tuesdays

I Dolci di Patrizio Cosi

Borgo degli Albizi, 15/r
055 2480367
Open 7AM—8PM, Monday to Saturday
Closed Sundays

Gelateria Alpina

Viale Filippo Strozzi, 12/r
(Fortezza da Basso)
055 496677
Open 6:45AM—9PM in winter
6:45AM—midnight in summer
Closed Tuesdays

Gelateria Veneta

Piazza Beccaria, 7/r
055 2343370
Open 8AM—8PM in winter
8AM—midnight in summer
Open daily

Hemingway

Piazza Piattellina 9/r
055 284781
Open 4:30PM—1AM,
Tuesday to Thursday
4:30PM—2AM, Friday & Saturday
11AM—8PM, Sunday
Closed Mondays

Marzocco

Via Cernaia 16/r
055 470581
Open 7AM—8PM
Closed 12PM—2PM,
Saturday & Sunday only
Open daily

Pasticceria Marino

Piazza San Domenico, 7/8
Fiesole (FI)
055 599716
Open everyday, 8AM—6PM

Perché No!

Via dei Tavolini, 19/r
055 2398969
Open noon—11PM, Wednesday to Monday
in winter
11AM—midnight, Wednesday to Monday
in summer
Closed Tuesdays

Ristorante Michelangelo

Viale Galileo Galilei, 2/r
(Piazzale Michelangelo)
055 2342705
Open 6:30AM—3:30AM, daily
Closed Wednesdays from November to February

Vivoli

Via Isola delle Stinche, 7/r
055 292334
Open 7:30AM—1AM, Tuesday to Saturday
9:30AM—1AM, Sunday
Closed Mondays